Cambridge Elements

Elements in Phonology
edited by
Robert Kennedy
University of California, Santa Barbara
Patrycja Strycharczuk
University of Manchester

SECOND LANGUAGE PHONOLOGY

Phonetic Variation and Phonological Representations

Ellen Simon
Ghent University

Shaftesbury Road, Cambridge CB2 8EA, United Kingdom

One Liberty Plaza, 20th Floor, New York, NY 10006, USA

477 Williamstown Road, Port Melbourne, VIC 3207, Australia

314–321, 3rd Floor, Plot 3, Splendor Forum, Jasola District Centre, New Delhi – 110025, India

103 Penang Road, #05–06/07, Visioncrest Commercial, Singapore 238467

Cambridge University Press is part of Cambridge University Press & Assessment, a department of the University of Cambridge.

We share the University's mission to contribute to society through the pursuit of education, learning and research at the highest international levels of excellence.

www.cambridge.org
Information on this title: www.cambridge.org/9781009663304

DOI: 10.1017/9781009420648

© Ellen Simon 2025

This publication is in copyright. Subject to statutory exception and to the provisions of relevant collective licensing agreements, no reproduction of any part may take place without the written permission of Cambridge University Press & Assessment.

When citing this work, please include a reference to the DOI 10.1017/9781009420648

First published 2025

A catalogue record for this publication is available from the British Library

ISBN 978-1-009-66330-4 Hardback
ISBN 978-1-009-42063-1 Paperback
ISSN 2633-9064 (online)
ISSN 2633-9056 (print)

Additional resources for this publication at www.cambridge.org/Simon

Cambridge University Press & Assessment has no responsibility for the persistence or accuracy of URLs for external or third-party internet websites referred to in this publication and does not guarantee that any content on such websites is, or will remain, accurate or appropriate.

Second Language Phonology

Phonetic Variation and Phonological Representations

Elements in Phonology

DOI: 10.1017/9781009420648
First published online: February 2025

Ellen Simon
Ghent University

Author for correspondence: Ellen Simon, Ellen.Simon@UGent.be

Abstract: This Element deals with the interplay between phonology, phonetics and acquisition. It addresses the question of whether and how phonological representations are acquired in adult second language (L2) learners in the face of phonetic variation inherent in speech. Drawing from a large number of empirical studies on the acquisition of L2 speech sounds, the Element outlines how phonetic or phonological representations develop in L2 learners on the basis of input in immersion and instructed language learning contexts. Taking in insights from sociophonetics and clinical linguistics, the Element further discusses how accent variation impacts L2 phonological acquisition and what clinical studies on individuals with atypical language development can tell us about the nature of phonological representations. Finally, new avenues in the field of L2 phonology are explored, especially with regard to methodological challenges and opportunities related to the use of spontaneous speech and remote data collection.

Keywords: second language phonology, sociophonetics, variation, phonological representations, perception

© Ellen Simon 2025

ISBNs: 9781009663304 (HB), 9781009420631 (PB), 9781009420648 (OC)
ISSNs: 2633-9064 (online), 2633-9056 (print)

Contents

1 Introduction	1
2 The Field of Second Language Phonology	4
3 Towards Robust Phonological Representations in a Second Language	7
4 Flexibility of Phonological Representations	14
5 Sociophonetics and Second Language Phonology	21
6 Fuzzy and Overspecified Representations	35
7 Assessing the Formation of Categories	40
8 Avenues for Future Research: How to Advance the Field of Second Language Phonology?	50
9 Conclusions and Implications	59
References	62

1 Introduction

Phonology is the study of sounds in languages. It is the field that is concerned with questions about which sounds in languages are used to contrast meaning, how sounds pattern together in terms of phonotactics (which sequences of sounds are permissible) and which phonological processes (such as assimilations or elisions) take place. Second language (L2) phonology, then, is the field that investigates how language users acquire the sound system of a language that is not their native or home language. The acquisition process in L2 phonology is fundamentally different from that in first language (L1) phonology, as L2 learners have already acquired the phonology of their native language, but now need to acquire a second sound system that is different from the one they had learnt from birth. Research has firmly established that this is not a trivial task: on a segmental level, for instance, many L2 learners struggle with the acquisition of sounds which are not contrastive in their native language. Moreover, prosodic differences, such as differences in rhythm, may pose additional challenges to the learner.

This Element focuses on the acquisition of L2 phonology at a segmental level, meaning at the level of consonants and vowels, and specifically discusses the impact of phonetic variation on the acquisition of an L2 phonological system. When native speakers of Dutch, for instance, are acquiring the sound system of English, they need to learn that the sounds /ɛ/ (as in 'bed'), and /æ/ (as in 'bad') are contrastive. As Dutch has only one vowel in this area of the vowel space, even the discrimination between these two English sounds and the perception of the sounds as distinct categories turn out to be challenges. Only with sufficient high-quality exposure may L2 learners succeed in building robust phonological representations in their L2. In addition, English sounds may be realized differently by different speakers of English, depending on, amongst other factors, the regional background of the speaker. In Australian English, for instance, the difference between the vowels /ɪ/ ('ship') and /i/ ('sheep') is spectrally reduced (Cox & Palethorpe, 2007). When L2 learners who have mostly been exposed to, for instance, American English, are then listening to an Australian English speaker, they need to adapt their perception to the accent of the speaker. Another example is the word 'better' produced in three different ways: with a plosive [t] and a final schwa by a speaker of British English (Speech sample 1), with a flap and a final [ɐ] by an Australian English speaker (Speech sample 2) and with a glottal stop and a ɐ, again by a speaker of Australian English (Speech sample 3). As shown in Figure 1, these three realizations of the same word differ considerably in terms of the acoustics of both the medial consonant and the final vowel. Despite this variability in the acoustic signal, listeners need to be able to map all three

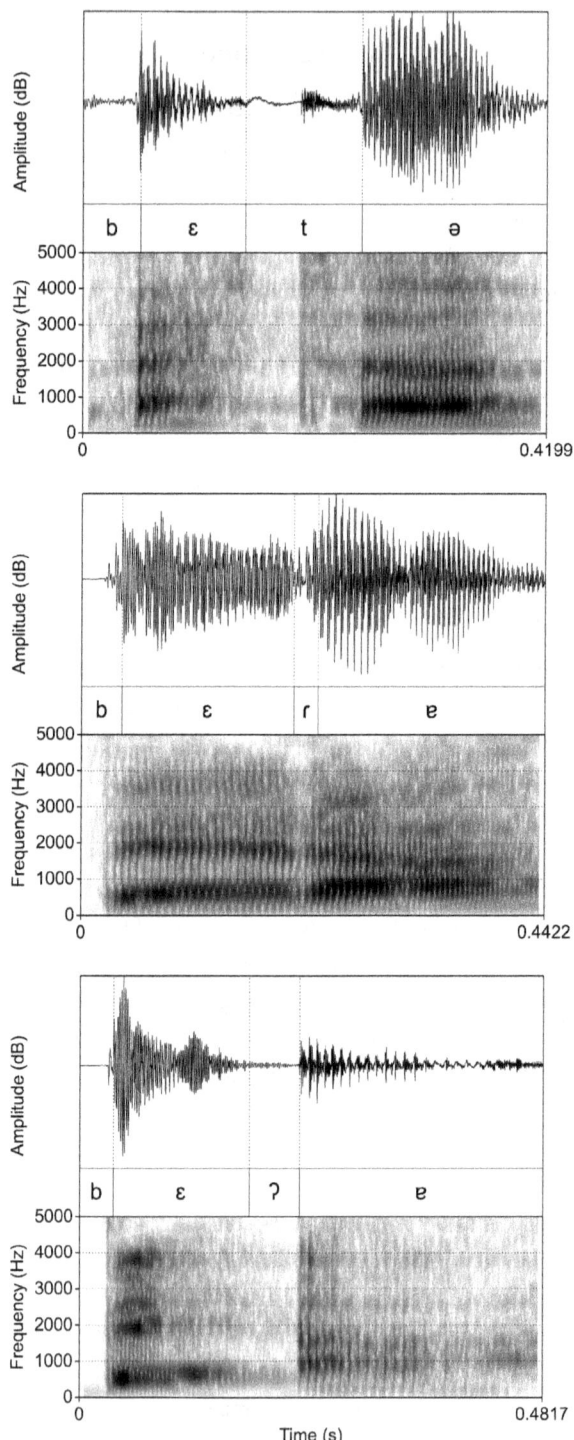

Figure 1 Different realizations of the word 'better' by a British English (top) and Australian English speakers (middle and bottom).

sounds to the same lexical item, 'better'. This is known as the 'lack of invariance' problem. This term was coined by Liberman et al. (1967) to refer to a long-standing issue in speech perception research which illustrates the complex relationship between acoustic cues and phonemes.

Speech sample 1 'better' with a plosive – British English speaker. Audio file is also available at www.cambridge.org/Simon
Speech sample 2 'better' with a flap – Australian English speaker. Audio file is also available at www.cambridge.org/Simon
Speech sample 3 'better' with a glottal stop – Australian English speaker. Audio file is also available at www.cambridge.org/Simon

This means that the learners' categories need to be sufficiently flexible to deal with all the variation that learners encounter. It is inherent that, whenever language learners come into contact with their target language, they are also automatically exposed to variation, including socio-indexical variation, which provides listeners with information on the regional and social background of the speaker. Despite this observation, relatively little research so far has addressed whether or to what extent L2 learners acquire sociophonetic information in an L2. As we will argue, the study of sociophonetic variation can enhance our understanding of how language users build phonological representations. Hence, insights from sociolinguistics and particularly from sociophonetics are relevant to the development of phonological theory. In addition, studies in clinical linguistics that focus on the phonology of atypically developing language users may provide further insight into the nature of phonological representations. If we come to understand whether – and if so, how – reduced language skills in this population can be related to phonological representations, insights from clinical linguistics may tell us something about how phonological representations are organized in typically developing L1 and L2 learners.

The Element centres around the following major topics:

- The field of L2 phonology (Section 2)
- The development of robust phonological representations in an L2 (Section 3)
- The flexibility of phonological representations (Section 4)
- The link between sociophonetics and L2 phonology (Section 5)
- Fuzzy and overspecified representations (Section 6)
- Assessing the formation of categories (Section 7)

In Section 8, avenues for future research will be explored as new ways to advance the field of L2 phonology in terms of methodology and theory. Conclusions are formulated in Section 9.

2 The Field of Second Language Phonology

2.1 A Field at the Crossroads of Different Disciplines

As noted in the introduction, scholars in the field of L2 phonology examine how language users acquire a phonological system in a language that is not their native or home language. The study of this acquisition process touches upon elements from different linguistic subdisciplines and requires insights from different domains, including L2 acquisition, phonological theory, phonetics and sociolinguistics, as visualized in Figure 2.

First, L2 phonology research is embedded in the field of L2 acquisition. In any type of language acquisition, three main types of 'actors' play a role: the learner, the context and the interlocutor or (target) recipient of the message that the learner wants to get across. A myriad of factors related to the learner impact the L2 learning process, including the learner's native language, age, age of first exposure, aptitude, motivation, length of residence in the country/region of the target language, amount of L2 use and socio-economic and educational background. The relative impact of these factors will depend on the context in which the learning process takes place. Important factors related to the context are the naturalistic versus instructed setting in which learning takes place, and the amount and quality of exposure, including the number of different interlocutors. Finally, there is a growing body of research on native listeners' perception of (L2) accented speech, comprehensibility (listeners' self-reported level of

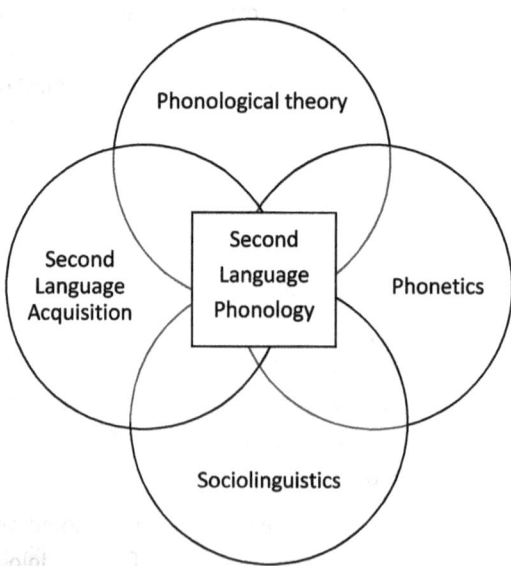

Figure 2 Second language phonology at the intersection of different disciplines.

understanding) and intelligibility (speech actually understood by the listeners). The speaker's pronunciation (segmental properties, prosody and fluency) and lexicogrammar (richness of vocabulary, as well as accuracy and complexity of grammar) have been shown to be the two main linguistic dimensions influencing a speaker's intelligibility and comprehensibility (Saito, Trofimovich & Isaacs, 2017). However, research on L2 phonology has increasingly recognized the impact of the interlocutor. Crucially, a learner's L2 speech can only be called (in)comprehensible or (un)intelligible *to a certain listener* (Munro, 2008; Simon, Lybaert & Plevoets, 2022). As a result, it is essential to recognize the role of the listeners in L2 phonological acquisition, including listener characteristics related to, for instance, native language, age, familiarity with L2 speech, social and sociopolitical attitudes, socio-economic status and educational background.

Secondly, in order to address issues in L2 phonology, questions that are fundamental to phonological theory need to be raised. Such questions can be related to the nature of phonological units, the way these units are organized and their level of abstraction. In order to build models of L2 phonological acquisition, the issue of what exactly needs to be learnt by the L2 speaker-listener needs to be addressed. When L1 learners start building phonological representations, they do so from scratch ('bottom up'), on the basis of phonetic input. Conversely, adult L2 leaners have a full set of L1 representations available, including their phonetic implementations. As a result, they may additionally use a 'top-down' approach in their processing of an L2, looking for correspondences between speech elements in their L1 and in the L2 (Flege, Munro & MacKay, 1995: 22).

Thirdly, research in L2 phonology draws on the field of phonetics, which is the science of how speech sounds are articulated, how they transfer through the air in the form of waveforms and what acoustic properties they have, and how they are perceived by the listener. Most current L2 speech acquisition studies start from the acoustic input: learners acquire an L2 sound system by being exposed to acoustic-phonetic forms (Flege & Bohn, 2021). As such, work in L2 phonology will necessarily draw on insights in the closely related discipline of phonetics. Much of the earlier work in laboratory phonology was devoted to the question of how phonology is related to phonetics (Cohn, Fougeron & Huffman, 2017) and this relationship remains a crucial factor in current discussions of L2 phonological research.

Finally, as variation is an inherent property of speech, one of the challenges faced by L2 learners is learning how to deal with this variation, which is at the same time linguistic and socio-indexical in nature. For instance, a vowel in a particular language may have different phonetic realizations, from more open to more closed and from more front to more back, depending on the flanking consonants (e.g. more fronted preceding a front consonant), but also on the speakers' regional or social backgrounds. When studying patterns of L2 phonological acquisition, we therefore also need to take into account insights from sociolinguistics, or – more specifically – from sociophonetics.

In sum, the field of L2 phonology is a discipline situated at the interface of research on L2 acquisition, phonology, phonetics and sociolinguistics. Non-native listeners need to build robust phonological representations in their L2, which can be impeded by their native language phonology (Section 3), different listening conditions (Section 4) or sociophonetic variation (Section 5). We will explore these challenges to L2 learning and zoom in on a group of learners that may help us to understand the nature and development of L2 phonological representations, namely child and adult atypically developing language users, who have been claimed to have fuzzy representations in their L1 (Section 6). In the next section (Section 2.2), we go back to a basic question in theoretical phonology that is key to the field of L2 phonology: what needs to be learnt?

2.2 What Needs to Be Learnt?

When people learn a language that is not their native language, they have to learn a new sound system. Even when the language they are learning is similar to their native language(s) in terms of, for instance, the grammar or the lexicon, there will undoubtedly be differences in the way in which segments are produced and interact with each other. The target language may have a sound that does not occur in the native language or not in the same positions (i.e. phonotactics may be different), it may have connected speech processes, such as assimilation patterns, which do not apply in the native language, or it may differ in the concrete realization of sounds. Hence, the question emerges what exactly needs to be learnt by learners who need to master the sound system of an L2. As Flege and Bohn (2021) point out, earlier speech learning models, such as contrastive analysis, made predictions regarding areas of difficulty in L2 acquisition, which were based on comparisons of the sound inventories at the *phonological* level: phonemes which did not occur in the L1 of the learner were predicted to be difficult. As these predictions were often not borne out, the idea that the *phonetic* level needs to be taken into account gained ground in the field of L2 speech acquisition research. Indeed, most current L2 acquisition studies now start from the acoustic input: learners are exposed – either in naturalistic or instructed settings – to acoustic-phonetic forms and acquire phonetic categories on the basis of this input. Most prevalent speech learning models – including the Speech Learning Model (SLM, Flege, 1995) and its revised version (SLM-r, Flege & Bohn, 2021), the Perceptual Assimilation Model (PAM, Best, 1995) and its adaptation for

L2 speech learning (PAM-L2, Best & Tyler, 2007) and the L2 Linguistic Perception Model (L2LP, Escudero, 2005) and its revised version (van Leussen & Escudero, 2015) – aim to account for how learners develop categories for L2 sounds on the basis of the phonetic input. In fact, in L2LP, it is even argued that a detailed acoustic comparison of L1 and L2 sounds can reliably predict L2 perception, since the acoustic properties of listeners' L1 speech sounds will be the starting point of initial L2 perception (Elvin, Escudero & Vasiliev, 2014). A useful overview of current speech learning and perception models including PAM, SLM, the Native Language Magnet Model and Automatic Selective Perception is provided by Chang (2019). Baese-Berk et al. (2022), focusing on perception, point out that most speech perception models rely on 'category learning'. They define a category as 'an abstract and generalizable representation that enables listeners to perceive highly variable acoustic input and efficiently process it through a more parsimonious representation with fewer perceptual dimensions than the raw sensory input' (3026).

Indeed, learners are exposed to a great deal of phonetic variation in the input and thus need to build representations at a more abstract level. In the next sections we aim to present a coherent overview of how this process takes place, how representations develop during the acquisition process and when the process may be hampered.

3 Towards Robust Phonological Representations in a Second Language

3.1 Developing Phonological Representations in First and Second Languages

Before we turn to the question of how L2 learners acquire L2 categories, it is interesting to consider how the process unfolds in L1 acquisition. After all, when adult language users learn an L2, the phonological system of their L1 will to a great extent determine the initial state of the L2 acquisition process.

Research on L1 acquisition has firmly established that after the first six months of life, children start to develop language-specific categories as a result of perceptual attunement to the native language (Kuhl, 1992; Polka & Werker, 1994; Werker & Tees, 1984; for a review, see Werker, 2018). This attunement is assumed to be the result of an increased knowledge of the phonological status of relevant L1 distinctions. In Kuhl's Perceptual Magnet Model (Kuhl, 1992), infants deduce this information through exploiting statistical properties, in the sense that highly frequent and hence familiar speech sounds would function as magnets by attracting similar sounds and thereby diminishing the discrimination between these similar sounds (Werker, 2018: 710). Throughout childhood and adolescence, speakers' phonological representations keep developing: as children grow older and turn into adolescents, the way in which they use acoustic cues while listening becomes more adult-like and perception gradually becomes more categorical. By the time they reach adulthood, they have normally built well-established, robust categories in their L1.

When adults then acquire an L2 they need to develop a new set of categories for the L2. A large body of research on L2 perception and word recognition has amply demonstrated that this is not a trivial task. In fact, acquiring new categories for contrasts which are absent in the L1 is known to be very difficult, even for highly proficient L2 learners. Examples are studies on the /r/-/l/ contrast in L2 English for L1 Chinese listeners (Aoyama et al., 2004; Cutler & Otake, 2004) or the /ɛ/-/æ/ contrast in L2 English for L1 Dutch learners (Broersma, 2005; Escudero, Simon & Mitterer, 2012; Simon, Sjerps & Fikkert, 2014). Previous research has, however, also established that L2 learners may be able to create new categories by shifting the boundaries of L1 categories in the direction of the L2 (Elman, Diehl & Buchwald, 1977; Flege & Eefting, 1987). According to models such as SLM-r and PAM-L2 (see Section 1), the likelihood of successful category creation is predicted to depend on the L2 category's relation to existing L1 categories. In SLM-r, the L2 sound's degree of perceived phonetic dissimilarity from the closest L2 sound will determine whether a new category is formed or not, in addition to the quantity and quality of L2 input and 'the precision with which the closest L1 category is specified when L2 learning begins' (Flege & Bohn, 2021: 65). In the framework, category precision is defined by the degree of acoustic variability that is produced by a speaker in multiple productions of the category. The authors refer to a study by Kartushina and Frauenfelder (2013), which showed that Spanish learners of French whose L1 Spanish /e/ productions were 'compact', in the sense of revealing relatively little token-to-token variability, were better at identifying French /ɛ/ than Spanish speakers with a less precise Spanish /e/ category – that is, in which there were more spectral differences between different /e/ realizations. Flege and Bohn (2021) point out that category precision is linked to the distance between the category and categories which are adjacent in phonetic space, but may also vary between different speakers, possibly as the result of differences in, for instance, auditory acuity and working memory (39).

As pointed out by Chang (2019), the L1 and L2 are linked not only at a segmental level, as predicted by SLM-r, but also at a broader, systemic level. Evidence for this comes from studies demonstrating the impact that an L2 can have on features of the L1, a process typically referred to as 'phonetic drift' (see also Section 8.2). Phonetic drift has been found in both immersion contexts (e.g. Chang, 2012, 2013 on English–Korean interactions in L1 English participants immersed in the L2 in South Korea) and in L1-dominant environments (e.g. Wojtkowiak, 2022 on the impact of L2 English on L1 Polish learners of English in Poland). On a segmental level, both vowels and consonants can be affected. An example of consonantal drift can be found in Sancier and Fowler's (1997) case study involving a female adult L1 Brazilian Portuguese speaker travelling back and forth between Brazil and the United States of America. An analysis of this person's speech revealed that her Brazilian Portuguese stops drifted towards those of American English during a stay in the US (in terms of Voice Onset Time (VOT)), while her English stops drifted towards those of Portuguese when in Brazil. However, phonetic drift has also been shown to occur at a level above the segment. Guion (2003) examined vowel qualities in the entire vowel inventory in a group of Quichua–Spanish bilinguals and found that bilinguals who had acquired Spanish produced Quichua vowels with an overall lower first formant – that is, more closed or higher in the vowel space. In a different context, Chang (2012) examined the English speech of a group of L1 English speakers who enrolled in elementary Korean classes and who were inexperienced, novice learners of the L2. Similarly to Guion's (2003) results, the acoustic analyses of the vowels revealed a general raising of the English vowels in this group of speakers. In neither of the studies could the drift be explained as shifts in individual vowels, as the L1 vowels did not all assimilate towards or dissimilate from the closest L2 vowels. Instead, Chang (2012, 2019) argues that the shift should be explained as the result of convergence towards the global formant levels of the L2, thereby transcending the level of the segment. Evidence for phonetic drift at the suprasegmental level can also be found in Mennen et al.'s (2022) study on the impact of L2 intonational patterns on the L1. Specifically, they examined different intonation dimensions in the English speech of adult L1 English migrants to Austria. The results showed that L2 intonation patterns impacted those in the L1, which exhibited values in between the L1 or the L2 or completely assimilated to the L2. These results demonstrate a lasting plasticity of the L1 intonation in late sequential bilinguals.

Together, studies on phonetic drift in L2 learners or sequential bilinguals provide evidence for a strong linkage between the L1 and the L2. They demonstrate that phonetic drift takes place on an allophone-to-allophone level, predicted by acoustic similarity and perceptual assimilation mappings, but also on a systemic level, including vocalic drift of the entire inventory or drift on a suprasegmental level. A comprehensive review of older and more recent phonetic drift literature can be found in an overview chapter by Chang (2019).

3.2 How Robust Is the Learning?

One of the long-standing issues in L2 phonological acquisition has been that of complete or ultimate attainment, which refers to the question of whether L2 learners can reach a level of phonological competence in the L2 that is similar to or the same as that of L1 native speaker-listeners. Discussions on this issue were often related to testing the critical period hypothesis. This hypothesis, proposed by Lenneberg (1967), states that there is a critical age after which full attainment of L2 phonology is impossible or – in milder versions of the hypothesis – more challenging, due to maturational changes in the brain. While the idea of a critical period is more readily accepted in the acquisition of an L1, it is less clearly outlined in L2 acquisition and several studies have provided compelling evidence against it (see, e.g., Zhang & Wang, 2007 on neural plasticity in speech acquisition). The hypothesis was tested in L2 acquisition studies comparing L2 learners' performance with that of native speakers and examining the effect of variables like the learner's age, motivation and the amount of instruction on the L2 performance (e.g. Moyer, 1999). After previously focusing on 'end state' learning in the original version of the SLM, the SLM-r argues that in order to examine whether L2 learners acquire new categories, studies should focus on the early stages of L2 acquisition rather than on highly experienced learners. Using production data by Italian immigrant learners in Canada, they argue that the patterns displayed by these learners indeed stabilize, but that 'this does not place an upper limit on the human capacity for learning speech when phonetic input changes' (Flege & Bohn, 2021: 28).

The ultimate attainment debate is now no longer central in L2 phonological acquisition research, but a related question that also lies at the basis of this debate is how far L2 learning actually goes. After all, if L2 learners can reach L1 levels of attainment, this implies that the L2 learning is as profound as L1 learning and that the phonological representations developed by L1 and L2 learners are equally robust. However, while researchers agree that L2 learners are – at least to some extent – able to acquire L2 speech sounds, there is as yet no consensus on how far the learning goes. Do L2 learners effectively create new, abstract categories or is the learning more superficial – that is, do learners temporarily shift some category boundaries when listening to L2 speech, without actually creating robust L2 categories that can be used in perception as well as in production? Barrientos (2021) addresses this question in her study on the perception of the American English vowel contrast between /ɑ/ ('cop' / kɑp/) and /ʌ/ ('cup' /kʌp/) by L1 Spanish listeners. The results showed that the advanced learners displayed an increased sensitivity towards acoustic properties relevant in the L2 and an improved discrimination between the two vowels.

However, the author argues that they did not develop a phonemic split at the representational level, meaning that the learning did not go far enough for the L2 listeners to develop two separate phonemes for /ɑ/ and /ʌ/. The claim is based on the absence of an S-curve in the L2 learners' vowel discrimination plots, which suggest that there are no two distinct phonemic representations at the end points to which vowels are categorically mapped.

Answers to the question of how robust L2 learning is can also be sought in training studies, in which L2 learners typically receive intensive phonetic training on L2 contrasts which are absent in the L1. A large number of empirical studies point towards the positive effect of such training sessions on perception and/or production, often using the High Variability Phonetic Training (HVPT) paradigm, in which listeners are exposed to multiple talkers (but see Zhang et al. 2021 and Xie, Liu & Jaeger, 2021, who address the question of whether multiple talkers are strictly necessary). However, questions about the robustness of these training effects have arisen, specifically about whether training leads to long-term effects on phonological representations or rather to short-term effects on perception. In a recent study (Simon, De Clercq et al., 2022), we examined the effects of multimodal HVPT sessions with two groups of adult L1 French learners of Dutch in Belgium: a group of university students and a group of final year secondary school students. The study focused on five Dutch sound contrasts which are absent in French – namely (1) /i/ vs /ɪ/, (2) /ɑ/ vs /a:/, (3) /ə/ vs ø, (4) /x/ vs /k/, and (5) /h/ vs ø. The design comprised a pretest, a post-test and a delayed post-test, with five training sessions as the intervention for the experimental group and no training for the control group. The training sessions consisted of perceptual identification tasks with feedback and metalinguistic information on Dutch sounds, including articulatory and acoustic information in the form of videos and waveforms. Specifically, we examined the robustness of the training effects, defined as the generalizability of the training to novel tokens and talkers, the effect of training in non-optimal conditions (i.e. with noise added to the signal), and – crucially – the long-term retention (Simon, De Clercq et al., 2022, in an edited volume on *Second Language Pronunciation*, Alves & Albuquerque, 2022). Long-term retention of learning is considered to be a signal that there have been long-term modifications to the phonetic or phonological categories as a result of the phonetic training (Rato & Oliveira, 2022). The results revealed variability along most robustness variables, which were to a large extent related to learner characteristics and type of L2 contrast. For instance, we observed training effects in the group of university students (on which most HVPT studies are based) along all three robustness variables, including long-term retention, but not in the group of secondary school pupils. This may have been related to the learners' proficiency levels or to their motivation to participate in the study. A systematic review of twenty-seven training studies which include the testing of generalization and/or retention is provided by Rato and Oliveira (2022), which appeared in the same edited volume. The authors conclude that all reviewed studies that tested generalizability (twenty-five out of twenty-seven studies) found carry-over effects to new stimuli, phonetic contexts, talkers and/or tasks. The same trend was observed for retention, which was tested in only eleven out of the twenty-seven papers. However, in only four out of eleven studies retention was reported for all conditions.

It should be noted that the HVPT paradigm represents one specific type of training, which is both supervised and attentive, in the sense that categories are made explicit as part of the training design. When participants are, for instance, trained on the different vowels in 'bed' and 'bad', the category labels are explicitly used during the training. This can be done through the use of the phonetic symbols (in this case /ɛ/-/æ/), through linking the phonemes to letters (e.g. <e> for /ɛ/ and <a> for /æ/), or through the consistent use of keywords representing the sounds (e.g. BED and BAD). In this kind of training, participants' attention is explicitly drawn to the contrastive speech sounds. However, learning can also take place in an unsupervised way by exposing learners to a large number of speech sounds whose distribution provides information on the categories. Chládková, Boersma and Escudero (2022: 1) define distributional learning as 'an unsupervised statistical learning mechanism that works through exposure to the probability distributions of speech sounds in one's environment'. They note that distributional learning was originally described as an unsupervised learning mechanism used by infants to develop categories for native speech sounds. Maye, Werker and Gerken (2002) conducted a laboratory study with American infants growing up in an English-speaking environment. The study showed that infants exposed to a bimodal distribution between a prevoiced [d] and a voiceless unaspirated [t], which both fall within the same native laryngeal category (English /t/), were better at discriminating between these two non-native categories compared to infants who had been exposed to a unimodal distribution during the training phase. Distributional learning paradigms have also been used with adults, with varying degrees of success, suggesting that adult learners may employ distributional learning to perceptually adapt to specific accents or to speech in noisy environments (for an overview of these studies, see Chládková et al., 2022). In their own study, Chládková et al. (2022) examined the effect of an unattended distributional training in the L1 on the creation of another boundary location between existing vowels (i.e. a shift of the boundary between /i/ and /e/ in Spanish) and on the creation of a new boundary (i.e. a new boundary between short and long vowels, which are not contrasted in Spanish). On the basis of neurological responses measured through electroencephalography (EEG), the authors concluded that perceptual learning took place in the case of boundary shift, but not (or hardly) in the case of a new boundary creation.

3.3 Concluding Remarks

In sum, adult L2 learners face a difficult task, as they have already built robust phonological representations in their L1 when they are first exposed to the sound system of an L2. The learners' task is particularly challenging when the L2 contains sound contrasts which are not phonemic in the L1, in which case learners need to create an additional category or categories. Although the task is challenging, research has demonstrated that (advanced) learners may be able to create new categories by shifting the boundaries of existing categories. Such shifts may take place as the result of continued exposure to L2 speech over an extended period of time and the process may be aided by a growing L2 vocabulary, as their perception will be guided by the lexicon (see Tyler, 2019 on phonological acquisition in the foreign language classroom). One way in which this learning process may be enhanced is through explicit phonetic training. Indeed, an accumulated body of research on L2 phonetic training suggests that phonetic (HVPT) training can lead to robust learning of non-native categories, which can be carried over to new contexts and talkers and which can be retained after a longer time period following the last training. However, a cautionary note is in place here: although there is now ample evidence that training *can* alter L2 listeners' perceptions, it is clear that it is by no means a trivial task. First, as discussed, long-term retention has been examined in only a small subset of training studies and is generally not found in all conditions – that is, for all groups and for all contrasts learners were trained on. Secondly, as noted by Rato and Oliveira (2022), there may be a bias in the training studies that get published. In all fields of research, experimental studies that do observe positive effects generally have a higher chance of being submitted and/or accepted for publication compared to studies that report null results of an intervention (Fanelli, 2012). This phenomenon is sometimes referred to as 'the file drawer effect', because the unpublished manuscripts are imagined to be gathering dust in researchers' desk drawers. Rato and Oliveira (2022) therefore suggest that it is in this context valuable to examine results in so-called grey literature, such as proceedings and unpublished reports.

In Section 4, we discuss how phonological representations need not only be robust, but also flexible, meaning that listeners can deal with the high variability in the phonetic realization of categories that they may be exposed to.

4 Flexibility of Phonological Representations

4.1 The Challenge of Variation: Non-optimal Listening Conditions

Variation is an inherent characteristic of spoken language and a listener hence needs to be able to flexibly adapt to varying acoustic signals. Speech variation comes in various forms and occurs at different levels, and not all types of variation present a challenge to the listener. In fact, most types of variation are generally completely unproblematic. For instance, a major type of variation that is inherent in any speech produced by more than one individual is due to anatomical differences between talkers. The acoustics of speech are largely formed by movements of the articulators in the vocal tract and by the size of the vocal tract and larynx. As the size of the vocal tract and larynx may considerably differ between speakers, the acoustic output will necessarily vary between talkers. For some automatic speech recognition and speaker verification models to work, these talker differences need to be cancelled out or normalized (Johnson, 2020). This is equally the case for linguistic studies that aim to compare, for instance, vowel formants across speakers. For that purpose, different mathematical models have been proposed to normalize vowels, some of which use vowel-internal and some vowel-external (i.e. comparison between vowels) normalization procedures. Another distinction is that between talker-intrinsic and talker-extrinsic normalization, in which data are normalized on the basis of one versus across multiple speakers (see, e.g., NORM: Vowel Normalization Suite 1.1, uoregon.edu). As Johnson (2020) points out, it remains an open question whether or not listeners use vocal tract length in speech perception. What is important from our perspective is, however, that listeners clearly have no difficulties with this type of variation and can map all the different acoustic outputs of these unique voices onto more abstract speech representations. In fact, listeners are extremely fast in detecting, for instance, speaker gender: a study by Owren, Berkowitz and Bachorowski (2007) showed that listeners are fairly accurate in speaker gender/sex judgements after exposure to less than 15 ms of speech. In a large-scale study including 100 adult voices and 618 listeners, Lavan (2023) showed that judgements on physical characteristics of talkers (age, gender and health) emerge fastest, after only 25 ms exposure, compared to traits ('trustworthiness', 'dominance', 'attractiveness'), and social characteristics ('educatedness', 'poshness', 'professionalism'), which are formed after 800 ms of exposure to single vowel productions.

However, other types of variation may pose difficulties even to native listeners. Conditions in which speech variation emerges that causes challenges for speech perception or speech recognition are sometimes called 'adverse conditions' (Guediche et al., 2014; Mattys et al., 2012) or 'non-optimal conditions'

(Simon et al., 2022). These adverse or non-optimal conditions can take multiple forms, depending on whether they relate to the source of speech, the environment or transmission of speech, or the receiver, as categorized by Mattys et al. (2012). Both source and environmental degradation lead to variation in the acoustic signal that reaches the listener. One interesting type of source gradation occurs when the speaker has an unfamiliar accent and produces 'accented speech', defined – following Munro and Derwing (1995a) – as speech that noticeably deviates from native speaker norms. By contrast, environmental degradation refers to distortions due to, for instance, noise resulting from competing talkers in the background or a noisy environment. Under both conditions, speech perception is more difficult compared to optimal listening conditions, in which the listener is familiar with the speaker's accent and the communication is set in a quiet environment. In the case of competing background talkers, a listener's brain is – to a greater or smaller extent depending on the individual – able to filter out irrelevant speech through selective auditory attention, a phenomenon commonly known as 'the cocktail party effect', a term coined by Cherry (1953; see also Kattner & Ellermeier, 2020). In the case of accented speech, by contrast, it is not the context that is responsible for the degradation of speech, but the speakers themselves. In that case, the deviations from the listener's norm will normally be systematic, in the sense that speakers will tend to deviate from the norm in similar ways, such as in the fronting of a vowel for which the listener expects to have a more posterior place of articulation or the substitution of a dental fricative by a stop. Even though there may be variability in the phonetic realization of particular segments in regional or non-native accented speech (e.g. Turner, 2024 on the production of French /u/ and /y/ by L1 English speakers), listeners are typically quite good at adjusting their perception to relatively systematic deviations from the expected realizations, a process commonly referred to as 'perceptual adaptation'.

4.2 L1 Listeners' Perceptual Adaptation to Accented Speech

When we are listening to speech, our perception is aided by our knowledge of the lexicon. An early study that provided evidence for this statement is the seminal work by Ganong (1980). In this study, listeners were exposed to auditory continua from, for instance, the word *task* to the non-word *dask*. Results revealed a significant lexical effect – that is, for ambiguous tokens, listeners showed a tendency to categorize sounds in such a way that the stimuli formed words rather than non-words. Two decades later, Norris, McQueen and Cutler (2003) were presumably the first to provide experimental evidence for the effect of lexical knowledge on perceptual learning. In their study, L1 Dutch listeners were first familiarized with Dutch words containing ambiguous realizations of either [f] (one group) or [s] (another group) as the final fricative. For instance, the /f/-final word 'witloof' (chicory) was realized as [wɪtlo?] and the /s/-final word 'naaldbos' (pine forest) was realized as [na:ldbɔ?], with [?] being a sound in-between [f] and [s]. The results of a subsequent phoneme categorization task revealed that listeners who had been trained on [f]-ambiguous words (type 'witloof') classified ambiguous tokens more often as [f], while the reverse pattern was true for the [s]-ambiguous group. A control group, who had been trained on *non-words* ending in an ambiguous fricative (and who could hence not be guided by lexical knowledge), showed a pattern intermediate between the two experimental groups, without a bias for either [f] or [s]. These results provide clear evidence that listeners in the experimental groups had used their lexical knowledge (e.g. that 'witloof', but not 'witloos' is a word in Dutch) and that lexical information is thus able to modify phonetic categorization and change the perceptual system.

The question which arises is what precisely happens when listeners adapt their perception to unfamiliar accents, be they regional, native or non-native accents. In exemplar-based models (see, e.g., an early publication by Johnson, 1997), episodic traces of talker- or context-specific elements are stored in the lexicon and retrieved when speech from the same talker or context is being processed. As such, as Dahan, Drucker and Scarborough (2008) point out, talker adaptation is an inherent part of such theories. By contrast, in theories that work with representations that have abstracted away from specific experiences with talkers or contexts, talker adaptation requires a temporary adjustment of these representations (Dahan et al., 2008: 711). In their study, Dahan et al. (2008) exposed American English listeners to an American English accent with which the participants were unfamiliar. In that accent, the vowel /æ/ is raised before a /g/ (as in 'bag'), but not before a /k/ (as in 'back'). Results showed that identification of /k/-final words was facilitated when participants had previously been exposed to /g/-words. In other words, perceptual adaptation took place even in the absence of exposure to the acoustic signal, suggesting that the absence of vowel raising in /k/-words was stored in the lexicon. The authors take these results to suggest that perceptual adaptation actually brings about at least a temporary adaptation of representations in the mental lexicon.

Bent and Baese-Berk (2021) discuss two main types of perceptual adaptation to non-native accented speech: the first involves the remapping of sound categories, the second the shifting of category boundaries. A remapping is necessary when the speaker substitutes one category by another one – for instance, when replacing English /θ/ by an alveolar plosive /t/ in words like *think* and *bath*. In that case, the listener needs to learn this rule and map the

[t] sound onto the phonological representation of the dental fricative. Shifting boundaries is necessary when the speaker makes a contrast between two categories, but places the boundary in a different position compared to native speakers. A typical example would be the placement of the VOT boundary between two laryngeal categories of stops. If native Dutch speakers transfer their laryngeal contrast into English, they would produce voiced plosives with pre-voicing and aspirated stops as short-lag ones (Simon, 2010). Native English speakers listening to Dutch-accented English would then need to shift the boundary of the voiceless plosive category from a high positive VOT to a VOT close to zero.

When exposed to accented speech, a listener thus essentially has to interpret the acoustic-phonetic signal in a new way, so that it is mapped onto the phonological category intended by the non-native speaker. The ease with which the listener performs this task may depend in part on the extent of familiarity of the listener with non-native accented speech. Studies on the effect of long-term linguistic experience with the perception of accented speech seem to show mixed results, as reviewed by Bent and Baese-Berk (2021). Kennedy and Trofimovich (2008) showed that English as a Second Language (ESL) teachers were better able to understand non-native accented speech compared to naïve listeners who reported little to no contact with L2 English speakers. Interestingly, the researchers manipulated the accented sentences in such a way that listeners could or could not rely on the lexical context. The results revealed that ESL teachers did not rely more on top-down information, such as the lexical context, but were in fact better at mapping the unexpected acoustic-phonetic signal onto the intended phonological representations, leading to a better word recognition. It should be noted that Kennedy and Trofimovich's (2008) study is based on a limited number (twenty-four in total) of participants. However, these findings tentatively suggest that if listeners are frequently exposed to non-native accented speech, their phonological representations become more flexible, in the sense that they become better at shifting the boundaries, expanding the boundaries or reweighing cues compared to listeners who are less frequently exposed to unfamiliar accents.

It is, in this context, noteworthy that in more naturalistic contexts, a high degree of exposure should be sufficient for perceptual adaptation to take place. When there is sufficient exposure and listeners have some time to adjust their perception to regular deviations from the expected norm, accented speech will not typically present a challenge to L1 listeners. For L2 listeners, by contrast, the situation may be different. In Section 4.3, we discuss why this may be the case.

4.3 The Double Challenge for Second Language Listeners

While native adult listeners are generally successful at adapting to speech in the face of variation in the acoustic signal, non-native listeners may experience more problems. Indeed, Mattys et al. (2012) mention an incomplete language model as one of the 'adverse conditions' in listening and argue that, leaving aside children who are still developing their L1 system, this case is best represented by non-native listeners, who have an incomplete knowledge of the language, not only at the phonological, but also at the lexical, morpho-syntactic, grammatical and idiomatic levels. As our literature review confirmed, perceptual adaptation by native listeners seems to be facilitated by, first, the lexicon and, second, by experience or familiarity. Since non-native listeners typically have a smaller vocabulary and are less familiar with the target accent, because they have received less naturalistic exposure, they are less aided by (most crucially) the lexicon or previous experience, compared to native listeners. That the lexicon plays a role in perception by (L2) listeners has been demonstrated in studies providing L2 listeners with subtitles while listening to non-native speech. A study by Mitterer and McQueen (2009), for instance, showed that L2 subtitles but not L1 subtitles facilitated the perception of unfamiliar Australian and Scottish accents by L1 Dutch listeners. Subtitles provide lexical information and when the subtitles were in the L2, they helped listeners with word recognition.

Although there seems to be consensus on the observation that listening to accented speech is generally more difficult in an L2, relatively little research has so far been carried out on whether or how L2 listeners deal with accented speech in the language they are learning. An exception is a recent study by Lee and Baese-Berk (2021), who examined whether non-native listener groups with different L1s adapted to L2 speech in a high- and low-variability talker condition. The results revealed that, first, L2 listeners showed adaptation to the American English accent after only limited exposure (as measured through reaction times on word recognition), and, second, that high variability in the sense of different talkers initially posed an additional processing cost for L2 listeners. However, in the end, exposure to multiple talkers enabled cross-talker generalization. An earlier study by Bruggeman and Cutler (2019) investigated perceptual adaptation to ambiguous speech sounds in the L1 (Dutch) and the L2 (English) of Dutch emigrants to Australia, who were all highly proficient in English and used Dutch with a limited group of relatives at home. The results revealed perceptual adaptation to novel L2 talkers, but not to novel L1 talkers. These findings suggest that perceptual adaptation to accented speech is possible, but flexibility needs to be *practised* through regular exposure to variation.

It should be noted that listening in an L2 is not always more difficult than listening in an L1, and that non-native listeners are not always disadvantaged compared to native listeners. Several studies have indeed reported an 'interlanguage speech intelligibility benefit' (henceforth ISIB), referring to a perceptual benefit when the speaker and the listener have the same L1 and hence share an interlanguage system, with similar L2 phonological representations. As discussed by Hayes-Harb et al. (2008), the ISIB can refer to two different situations. First, some studies have demonstrated that non-native listeners are equally good or better at perceiving non-native speech compared to native speech, if the listeners share an L1 with the non-native talkers. Hayes-Harb et al. (2008) refer to this as a benefit for talkers, or ISIB-T. For instance, Bent and Bradlow (2003) conducted a study on the perception of English speech produced by L1 English, L1 Chinese and L1 Korean talkers. The listeners had either English, Chinese, Korean or a set of other languages as their L1. The results of a sentence transcription task showed that the relative intelligibility of each talker depended on the language background of the listeners. Crucially, non-native talkers with the same L1 as the listeners were equally intelligible to these listeners as native talkers. Secondly, non-native listeners may have an advantage over native listeners when listening to L2 speech that is produced by a speaker with whom they share an L1, a process referred to as ISIB-L: a benefit for listeners. Evidence for ISIB-L was found by, among others, Hayes-Harb et al. (2008), who analysed the perception of Mandarin-accented English speech by L1 English and L1 Mandarin Chinese listeners. They found that English speech produced by low-proficiency talkers was more intelligible (as measured through a forced-choice identification task) to low-phonological-proficiency listeners of L1 Mandarin Chinese, compared to L1 English listeners. To conclude, while there is sufficient evidence to claim that an ISIB can take place, both for listeners and for talkers, it is worth pointing out that it certainly cannot always be observed and that it seems to be modulated by factors such as talker and listener phonological proficiency and degree of accentedness (Fishero, Sereno & Jongman, 2023; Xie & Fowler, 2013).

As mentioned, another type of listener with a yet incomplete language system is children whose L1 is still developing. Just like non-native listeners, child native listeners have a smaller vocabulary and less experience with the target language compared to adult native listeners. Research on perceptual adaptation in child native listeners has demonstrated that by the age of twenty-eight months, toddlers can recognize words and sentences produced in an unfamiliar dialect, even without prior exposure to the dialect (van Heugten & Johnson, 2016). Bent and Baese-Berk (2021) discuss the question of what precisely children do when they adapt to these unfamiliar accents: do they apply rules specific to the accented speech of the talkers, or do they apply general expansion rules, loosening up the criteria for category membership? A study by White and Aslin (2011) seems to suggest the former, as children were – after exposure – successful in recognizing words with shifted vowels and could generalize to words with similar vowel shifts, but were not more liberal in accepting deviant pronunciations in general. However, as pointed out by Bent and Baese-Berk (2021: 445), children (and adults) may use different strategies in lab experiments commonly used to examine perceptual adaptation compared to more naturalistic exposure to longer stretches of non-native speech. In more naturalistic non-native speech, there is never just one deviating feature, such as a vowel shift, but rather a cluster of features that differ from the default. In such circumstances, it is possible that listeners would apply more general strategies in which they relax the membership criteria in order to cope with the accented speech. This latter view is taken by Melguy and Johnson (2021) in their study on L1 adult listeners who were presented with Chinese-accented English speech. American English listeners were asked to transcribe Chinese-accented sentences in noise and were assigned to different visual conditions: a blank silhouette, a European face, an East Asian face or a South Asian face. Participants who believed the speaker to be non-natively accented significantly outperformed participants who reported to hear a native accent, but no advantage was observed for listeners who correctly identified the speaker as Chinese-accented compared to other foreign accents. The authors suggest that these results point in the direction of a general relaxation of category boundaries or a general expansion of categories. The results of another study by the same authors (Melguy & Johnson, 2022) point in the same direction: listeners trained on ambiguous sounds showed a general category expansion, though this expansion proved to be limited by phonetic similarity – that is, if the sounds in testing were too dissimilar from the ones in training, listeners did not include them in the target category.

4.4 Concluding Remarks

In sum, although non-optimal listening conditions may require temporal adjustment by native listeners or may slow down speech recognition, they often present little actual challenge to intelligibility thanks to listeners' rapid perceptual adaptation. This is especially true for variation resulting from talker-specific characteristics, regional accents or mildly non-native accented speech. For more strongly accented non-native speech, listeners can also improve their understanding, but gains may be more modest. As noted by Bent and Baese-Berk (2021), these results point towards the flexibility of the perceptual system, but also to the remaining existence of differences in the extent to which non-native speakers are intelligible.

When L2 learners listen to either regionally or non-native accented speech, they may be doubly burdened: they need to map the L2 sounds onto the intended categories, which may differ from their L1 categories, and they need to adjust their expectations about the phonetic realizations of these L2 categories on the basis of the input. Whether L2 listeners apply certain rules when listening to accented speech, such as shifting the boundary between particular vowels, or apply general expansion rules, relaxing the criteria for category membership, is a matter in need of further investigation.

In Section 5, we delve a little deeper into the matter of accent variation and more generally discuss what the study of social and regional language variation brings to the field of L2 phonology.

5 Sociophonetics and Second Language Phonology

5.1 Sociophonetics and Phonological Theory: Is There a Match?

Sociolinguistically relevant similarities and differences between accents of different speakers and speaker communities form the object of study in the field of sociophonetics, a discipline at the interface between sociolinguistics and the phonetic study of speech and one that is currently a growing area of new research (see Kendall et al., 2023 for an overview of recent advancements in the field). Foulkes and Docherty (2006: 411) define sociophonetic variation as 'variable aspects of phonetic or phonological structure in which alternative forms correlate with social factors', which 'include most obviously those social categories which have been examined extensively by sociolinguists and dialectologists: speaker gender, age, ethnicity, social class, group affiliations, geographical origin, and speaking style'. Whenever we listen to speech, we derive not only linguistic, but also socio-indexical information: these are invariably present together in any utterance. For instance, when listening to the speaker in Speech sample 4, listeners will deduce that the speaker is male and many will also be able to identify his accent as Southern American English. Similarly, many listeners will hear that the speaker of Speech sample 5 is not a native speaker of English and some will deduce from the speech signal that his native language is Spanish. Finally, segmental as well as prosodic features in Speech sample 6, taken from the Phonologie du français contemporain (PFC) corpus, may allow listeners to identify this French speaker as coming from the Marseille region in the south of France. Coquillon (2007) contains a detailed discussion of phonetic features in this speaker's speech that are typical for Marseille French, such as the long nasal vowels ending in a nasal consonant.

Speech sample 4 Southern American English
'You feel the pressure, right, because you you've got fans that are wanting you to keep doing it. And then a lot of times people that are in the industry,

they think that everybody else out in the world wants their job, right.' (see Verbeke & Simon, 2023b for replication data). Audio file is also available at www.cambridge.org/Simon

Speech sample 5 Spanish-accented English
'Honestly, it's a, it's a big pleasure, because, uh, we enjoyed a lot of good experiences together, working together with my friend. Now be able to be here expanding [...] the, the brand here in, in Australia is something that uh I am super happy, you know, and be part of.' (see Verbeke & Simon, 2023b for replication data). Audio file is also available at www.cambridge.org/Simon

Speech sample 6 Southern French
'Alors je suis un peu le, le lien entre toutes les personnes, j'essaie de euh, j'essaie de calmer les, les esprits quand ça s'échauffe, et puis bon.' Audio file is also available at www.cambridge.org/Simon

As noted by Kendall and Fridland (2021), the field of sociophonetics is necessarily empirical, but is driven by broad questions which are deeply rooted in the field of linguistics, such as:

> 'How do speakers and listeners make use of speech variability (a squarely sociolinguistic question) and (its psycholinguistic analog) how do speakers and listeners cope with the great extent of speech variability?' (Kendall & Fridland, 2021: 5)

By addressing such questions, it is argued, sociophonetic studies may be able to build a bridge between empirically driven analyses of speech and cognitive-linguistic questions about the production and perception of speech. As Thomas (2013) notes, '[e]xperiments involving sociolinguistic variants can also be used to test the cognition of phonology' (110). Foulkes and Docherty (2006) highlight the minor role sociophonetics has played in the development of phonological theory. But how easy is it to actually make the link between sociophonetics and phonological theory? Which sociophonetic experiments can be set up to get insight into language users' phonological system?

In a review paper, Foulkes and Docherty (2006) assess to what extent sociophonetic studies can inform theory building in phonetics and phonology. They argue that traditionally, social factors, responsible for differences between speakers, have not been included in studies aimed at advancing our knowledge of phonology. They ascribe this exclusion to the influence of generative-based models, in which an ideal speaker-hearer is assumed and variation is considered irrelevant for theory building (see Goldrick & Cole, 2023 for a discussion). However, usage-based approaches in the framework of exemplar theory may be more apt at dealing with sociophonetic variation. Thomas (2013) suggests that sociophonetic experiments on style-shifting and the intelligibility of dialects 'could help resolve the extent to which Exemplar Theory accounts for phonological cognition' (122), though exactly how the link should be made is left to explore.

Exemplar-based models of memory have a long history in cognitive psychology, but have been proposed for the study of language for some decades as well now (Johnson, 2007). As Johnson (2007) points out, there is no one 'Exemplar Theory', but rather different exemplar-based models, which have in common that they rely on the assumption that language users store traces of all the instances they encounter in their memory without any abstraction. As these instances or exemplars (or traces thereof) are stored with detailed phonetic information, exemplar-based approaches to phonology are often considered to be suitable frameworks for modelling sociophonetic variation. In exemplar-based models, acoustic input is processed by comparing it to previously encountered stimuli with which the new input is compared. As a consequence, *frequency* of exposure and *recency* of exposure are crucial elements in these usage-based learning models (Frisch, 2017). As the relation between linguistic form and sociophonetic variation is arbitrary, language users indeed need to be exposed to the variation to a sufficient degree and the exposure needs to be sufficiently recent. As type and amount of exposure to particular categories of phonetic variation – such as different accents – will differ over a language user's lifespan, it may mean that the 'representation of phonological knowledge may be less stable, even in adulthood, than is typically assumed' (Foulkes & Docherty, 2006: 434). However, if one assumes a hybrid model, in which there are two layers, there may be one layer with stable phonological knowledge, and one layer with flexible forms, ever-changing as exposure and frequency of exposure change. Such a model is proposed by Pierrehumbert (2016), who argues that an abstract level of representations is needed in phonology to account for language users' ability to generate and process novel forms, but needs to be complemented by detailed phonetic characteristics. Phonetic characteristics of words are highly variable, as they are affected by several context effects. Such contextual factors include the position of the word in the phrase relative to the element that receives phrasal stress, the frequency and predictability of the word in a phrase, the individual speaker's anatomical and dialectal features, as well as social context factors, such as the speaker's social class or register within a particular social context (Pierrehumbert, 2016). As Pierrehumbert (2016) argues, '[t]he ability to perceive indexical features, produce them more or less in different contexts, and generalize them to new words and new interlocutors means that they must be cognitively represented' (43). If they are cognitively represented and stored in memory, they need to be part of phonological theory.

A theory assuming abstract phonological representations does then not need to be incompatible with a usage-based model. Instead, a hybrid model is needed which works with a layer of abstract representations complemented with detailed phonetic information signalling indexical properties.

5.2 Acquiring Sociophonetic Information

A usage-based approach to the storage and processing of speech has implications for models of language learning, both as an L1 and as an L2. As Foulkes and Docherty (2006) point out, 'the interweaving of sociophonetic and linguistic information in speech is so complete that no natural human utterance can offer linguistic information without simultaneously indexing one or more social factor' (419). Therefore, an acquisition or learning model in which both types of information are processed and stored together is desirable. In the next sections, we review research on the acquisition of socio-indexical features in an L1 by children acquiring their native language and by adults moving to a new dialect region, before turning to the question of how L2 learners gain knowledge of sociophonetic information in an L2 and acquire L2 sociophonetic features in perception and production.

5.2.1 Social, Attentional or Linguistic Biases in First Language Acquisition

The first time language users receive sociophonetic information is, of course, when acquiring their native language as infants. In fact, Foulkes and Hay (2015) point out that there is evidence that sociophonetic acquisition even starts in utero, as the developing baby can hear sounds from outside the womb and will learn to associate specific speech characteristics with the voice of the mother.

As mobility increases, children are more and more often exposed to different accents, including both unfamiliar regional accents and non-native ones. Johnson, van Heugten and Buckler (2022) review how children acquiring their native language develop in the way they deal with accent variation from infancy to toddlerhood. Earlier research has shown that from the age of about five months onwards, infants are able to perceive the difference between their own variety of the native language and an unfamiliar one. For instance, Nazzi, Jusczyk and Johnson (2000) showed that five-month-old infants acquiring American English as their native language can tell American and British English apart. In addition, eleven- to twelve-month-old infants demonstrate preferences for speakers with a native as opposed to a non-native accent, by being, for instance, more likely to try foods introduced by speakers from a native as opposed to a foreign language. As pointed out by Johnson et al. (2022), these biases may be attentional rather than social, in that they may indicate that infants around the age of twelve months have identified accent as a cue to group membership. Alternatively, the biases may be cognitive or linguistic in nature, arising from a preference for communication ease, which is presumably higher with familiar than with unfamiliar accents (Johnson et al., 2022: 369). In any case, it is not until children are approximately nineteen months old that they can reliably recognize familiar words produced in unfamiliar accents (e.g. van Heugten et al., 2018). Before that age, children struggle to recognize such words without previous exposure. When children are briefly – a few minutes, for instance – exposed to an unfamiliar accent before testing, they seem much better able to process familiar words in the unfamiliar accent. This positive effect of exposure has even been observed for children of only fifteen months (van Heugten & Johnson, 2014).

When children are about two years old, we observe a sudden significant increase in their ability to process unfamiliar accents. However, well into adolescence, children are outperformed by adults on comprehension or repetition tasks involving unfamiliar accents (Johnson et al., 2022). The question then arises to what extent the quick increase in children's ability to deal with accent variation around the age of two may be due to developing phonological representations and to what extent the children's struggles to keep up with the adults until adolescence may be an indication of incomplete acquisition of phonological representations. Johnson et al. (2022) forward the 'hybrid flexibility hypothesis', which basically combines the expansion hypothesis and the specific mapping hypothesis: initially children are thought to employ a general expansion approach when they are confronted with unfamiliar word forms (e.g. 'fish' pronounced as [fiːʃ]), meaning that they loosen up category membership criteria (so that [fɛʃ] would also be accepted). As they acquire more and more words, however, and their lexical and phonological representations become more fixed, children start to apply a specific mapping approach, meaning that when confronted with a word in an unfamiliar accent, children adjust the specific mapping between the prelexical and the lexical level – that is, they would adjust the mapping of [iː] to /ɪ/, but not the mapping of [ɛ] to /ɪ/, to which they have not been exposed. As Johnson et al. (2022) point out, specific mappings are only established after sufficient exposure, so that 'children's lexical representations necessarily need to contain abstract phonological detail for this account to work' (377).

5.2.2 Second Dialect Acquisition by Adults: The Interplay between Social and Linguistic Factors

As the review in Section 5.2.1 shows, there is a growing body of research on the acquisition of sociophonetic information by children learning their L1. By contrast, few studies have investigated the process in adults learning an L2.

We therefore first turn to a related question, namely to what extent adults learn to identify and distinguish between different dialects in their L1. Also in adulthood, language users may come into contact with speakers of unfamiliar accents. The result of increased mobility is that listeners in particular areas are exposed to various accents of mobile speakers who enter their community. However, the geographically mobile speakers themselves are also impacted: as these people move to a different region or country where their native language is spoken, they are exposed to and may eventually acquire aspects of a second dialect within their native language. Studies in the field of second dialect acquisition may be particularly suited to address questions about the acquisition of phonetic and phonological representations, as second dialect learners need to acquire new speech sounds without having to acquire a new lexicon. This makes their acquisition process ideal for the study of the relationship between abstract representations and phonetic realizations (Nycz, 2015). In her paper on the acquisition of a second dialect by native speakers of English, Nycz (2013) examines the acquisition of two properties of the New York City region accent by native speakers of Canadian English who moved to the United States of America after the age of twenty-one. Specifically, they investigate whether the participants acquired the cot /ɑ/ – caught /ɔ/ vowel distinction absent in Canadian English (where these vowels are merged to /ɑ/), and lost the 'Canadian raising' in the /aʊ/ diphthong (the raising of the starting point of the diphthong before voiceless consonants). The results of acoustic analyses of vowels produced in naturalistic, one-on-one interviews showed that speakers had shifted their vowels in the direction of the L2 dialect for both features in a lexically and phonetically gradient way: not all words were equally affected and the shift was gradient and mostly small. According to Nycz (2013), these findings are in line with usage-based approaches, as generative approaches would predict abrupt phonetic changes in all lexical items at once. In order to account for the observation that Canadian raising was strongly present in the speakers' spontaneous speech, Nycz argues that exemplars must be tagged for social characteristics. If exemplars with raised diphthongs are tagged as salient, typically Canadian realizations, speakers (especially those with a high linguistic sensitivity) may retain this feature in their speech when talking about their lives as Canadian expats in the US, which was the topic of the interviews. Such an account is in line with other second dialect acquisition research. For example, Evans and Iverson (2007) studied native speakers of northern British English attending universities in different parts of England, where they came into contact with varieties of southern British English, which is considered the more prestigious variant. The students' vowels were measured at various points over the course of two years, before their start of university, three months later and at the end of their first and second years at university. Results of vowel measurements in the students' speech revealed that speakers' vowels in words like 'strut' and 'foot', which in northern accents are merged to /ʊ/, were gradually realized with a more centralized, /ʌ/-like quality. In other words, the speakers did not produce a split between /ʌ/ and /ʊ/, as would be expected in southern English, but did produce phonetically gradient realizations in the direction away from a salient northern English accent.

As Nycz (2013) points out, the extent to which mobile adults – temporarily or more permanently – adapt their accent to that of speakers of a different dialect will not only be determined by social factors, such as the degree to which a speaker identifies with the local community, but also by linguistic ones, such as the form of phonological representations and their malleability. As such, second dialect data can answer fundamental questions about the nature of phonological representations.

5.2.3 Metalinguistic Knowledge and Intelligibility of Second Language Accents

We then turn to the population that is the focus of this Element: adult L2 learners. When individuals learn an L2, they need to acquire both linguistic and indexical features, just like in their L1. Long, Fox and Jacewicz (2016) define indexical information as pertaining to 'those aspects of variability in speech that are co-present with the linguistic information and that cue both biological and social attributes about a talker, such as age, sex, regional dialect or foreign accent, emotional state, or socioeconomic background' (901).

Acquiring metalinguistic knowledge of sociophonetic variation in an L2 is essential for learners to gain communicative competence. The field of L2 sociophonetics takes to heart the question of how language learners acquire socially relevant information in an L2. As Gnevsheva (2022) notes, this subfield is still relatively small, but as the body of work in sociophonetics is growing, the number of studies on the acquisition of sociophonetic information in an L2 will equally increase.

The earliest work on the acquisition of sociophonetic knowledge in an L2 is a study by Eisenstein (1982), which points at the important role of linguistic experience in the L2. Eisenstein's (1982) study, reviewed by Clopper and Bradlow (2009), deals with the perception of different dialects of English by native and non-native English listeners in New York City. The results revealed that the more advanced English learners outperformed the beginning and intermediate learners in discriminating between the different dialects and in fact reached native listener levels of discrimination. The higher performance of the advanced learners can presumably be attributed to their longer or larger exposure to linguistic and social features of the L2. Similarly, Stephan (1997) found that L1 German listeners' accuracy in identifying different World English varieties differed considerably across dialects, which he attributed to the different degrees of exposure to these varieties in German EFL classrooms.

As noted by Clopper and Bradlow (2009), classifying and discriminating between different dialects in an L2 requires the learners to master two sets of skills: (1) sensitivity to fine (i.e. sub-lexical) phonetic contrasts in the L2, and (2) knowledge of the set of (arbitrary) phonetic properties that together make up the dialect. The authors used a free dialect classification task in which native and non-native listeners were asked to group speakers of varieties of English according to their dialect, without having to provide labels. The results of two experiments with discrete categorical (consonantal) features (Experiment 1) and gradient (vowel) features (Experiment 2) revealed that the non-native listeners were able to use these acoustic properties as signals of dialect group membership – that is, they were able to distinguish between different clusters of accents, though they were less accurate than the native listeners in clustering the dialects together. The results of Experiment 2 additionally showed that the non-native listeners sometimes relied on cues in their L1 which are not relevant in the L2 to classify dialects and, reversely, sometimes ignored relevant cues in the L2. That the L1 plays an important role in the perception of socio-indexical features in an L2 should come as no surprise, given the generally acknowledged importance of L1 influence on the perception of L2 speech (cf. PAM and SLM; see Section 3.1).

Clopper and Bradlow (2009) argue that linguistic experience with different dialects may not only have an effect on dialect discrimination or identification, but also on intelligibility. They refer to a study by Fox and McGory (2007), which showed that both native English and Japanese listeners were better at identifying vowels produced in General American, compared to Southern American, showing an intelligibility benefit for the acrolectal variety.

More recently, we examined the comprehensibility, accentedness and intelligibility of eight varieties of English by a group of Dutch-speaking EFL learners (Verbeke & Simon, 2023a). While comprehensibility and accentedness were assessed through scalar ratings of speech samples, intelligibility was measured as accuracy rate on a sentence transcription task. The results revealed that speakers with Inner Circle accents (both acrolectal General American and General British and regional, in this case Texan English and Newcastle UK), were reported to be more comprehensible than what are traditionally referred to as Outer and Expanding Circle accents (cf. Kachru's model of World Englishes, 1985). No correlation was observed between comprehensibility and intelligibility.

Intelligibility was highest for General American, which may be explained by the great exposure of Flemish pupils to this variety through popular media. Self-reported familiarity with the different varieties was not a significant predictor of comprehensibility, but this may be due to the observation that familiarity was relatively similar among participants, with a high degree of familiarity reported for, for instance, General American and British English and a low familiarity with Indian and Nigerian English.

However, that the relation between linguistic experience and the perception of different regional dialects is complex is demonstrated in a study by Alcorn et al. (2020) on the classification of regional dialects in American English listeners' native language. The results of a free classification task involving sixty speakers of six different American English accents, all producing the same sentence, revealed that the two listener groups, from Ohio and Texas, were not better at grouping talkers from their own dialect. In addition, listeners who had been geographically mobile and had resided in several regions did not outperform listeners who had resided in one single area.

In sum, it has become clear that whether we are talking about L1 acquisition, second dialect or L2 acquisition, the rate and extent of the acquisition of indexical knowledge appears to strongly depend on the amount and recency of exposure or linguistic experience. Although the relationship between these variables is complex and in need of further research, it seems safe to conclude that the acquisition of indexical information remains incomplete if language users are insufficiently exposed to the specific type of variation. As noted by Foulkes and Docherty (2006), 'Clopper's (2004) evidence that adults have relatively poor ability to recognize regional or social or ethnic accents with any degree of precision underlines the fact that strongly arbitrary and/or low frequency socio-indexical patterning may never be fully mastered' (429–430). In Section 5.2.4, we zoom in on the acquisition of sociophonetic features in L2 accents.

5.2.4 Acquisition of Second Language Accent Variation

Besides gaining metalinguistic knowledge of accent variation in an L2, necessary for accent recognition, L2 learners also need to acquire sociophonetic features in both perception and production. Research has shown that the learning process may be impacted by the acquisition of accent variation in an L2. One type of perceptual issue mentioned by Thomas (2013) that can be addressed in sociophonetic studies is the question of 'how dialectal differences affect the phonological categorization of phones (Janson 1983), as the boundaries may differ by dialect' (121). If this question is relevant for L1 users, it certainly also pertains to L2 users who are exposed to different regional and social accents in the L2. The variation in the L2 may manifest itself in two different target accents, as in the study by Escudero and Boersma (2004), who looked at the differential vowel acquisition by L1 Spanish listeners of L2 Southern British English and Scottish English. However, multiple accents may also be present in the target language to which learners are exposed, as is, for instance, the case for many EFL learners in Europe, who are exposed to both British and American English accents.

While studies on L1 perception have convincingly shown that listeners are especially apt at dealing with regional variation in their native language (Bent & Baese-Berk, 2021; Dahan et al., 2008), the extent to which L2 listeners deal with different accents in the L2 has been investigated much less. In a recent study (Simon, De Clercq & Degrave, in prep.), we examined the perception of two Belgian Dutch accents by L1 Dutch listeners and L1 French learners of Dutch in Belgium. The accents compared were the acrolectal Standard (Belgian) Dutch accent and the regional Antwerp accent. Since L2 listeners have fewer higher-order resources to rely on when exposed to unfamiliar accents and since their phonological representations may not be robust enough to be flexible, the prediction was that L2 learners would be less apt at dealing with regional variation in the L2 compared to L1 listeners. The results, however, revealed that the French listeners did not experience more difficulty in the categorization or transcription of regionally accented vowels than Standard Dutch vowels, though they were outperformed by native listeners in both tasks (see Figure 3).

In addition, we predicted that participants would perform better in the transcription task, in which they were exposed to longer stretches of speech, than in the categorization task. The prediction was based on the fact that longer stretches of speech contain more acoustic-phonetic information and thus opportunities for listeners to familiarize themselves with and adapt to the unfamiliar regional accent. However, the results of a mixed linear regression model did not reveal any task effects (Simon et al., in prep.). Our results suggest that regional accents are not necessarily more problematic for L2 listeners than standard, acrolectal accents. Rather, the type of acoustic cues signalling phonemic contrasts and the correspondences between L2 and L1 vowels seem to be more important in the listeners' success at identifying vowels than the standard versus regional accentedness per se. Chappell and Kanwit (2022) examine the role of L2 proficiency, study abroad experience and explicit instruction on L2 Spanish learners' acquisition of a specific phonetic variable, namely coda /s/ reduction (e.g. esquina, 'corner', realized with [h] instead of [s]), which occurs in large parts of the Spanish-speaking world (e.g. Caribbean, Central and South America and southern Spain) and is a salient marker of regional and social

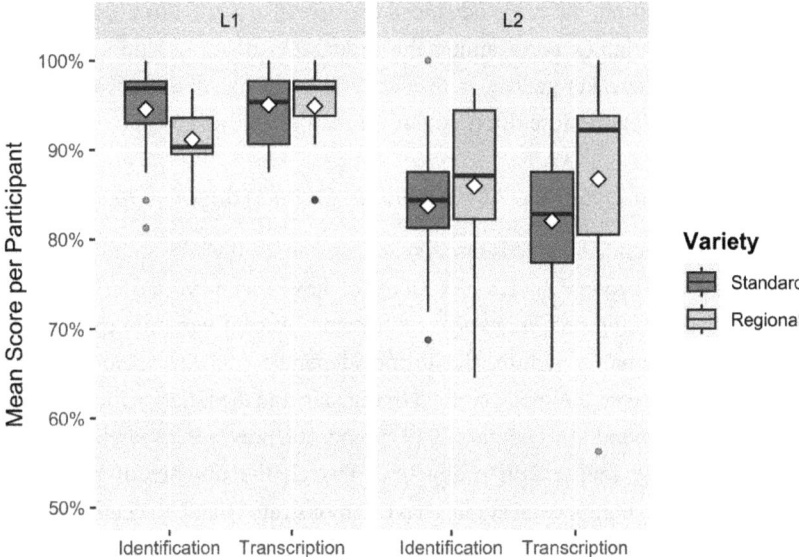

Figure 3 Boxplots representing average scores per participant for the L1 group (left plot) and L2 group (right plot) on the categorization and transcription tasks (Simon et al., in prep.).

identity (Chappell & Kanwit, 2022: 189). They observed that more proficient learners more often linked /s/ reduction to regional origin and social status than less advanced learners. Additionally, participants who had taken a phonetics course in which their attention was explicitly drawn to regional variation in /s/ reduction, and participants who had spent time studying Spanish abroad in a community in which /s/ reduction is produced more often identified this feature as typical for Caribbean Spanish.

Solon and Kanwit (2022) similarly examined the acquisition of Spanish intervocalic /d/ deletion, in words like 'cantado' ('sung'), realized as [kantao] (cf. also Solon, Linford & Geeslin, 2018). The form with deletion is widespread in the Spanish-speaking world, though deletion rates reported for different varieties range from 10 per cent to almost 40 per cent (Solon & Kanwit, 2022: 810). Particularly male speakers and individuals of lower socio-economic status have been reported to produce the variant with deletion. American English learners of Spanish performed a contextualized preference task in which they heard a male and female speaker of Colombian Spanish produce sentences with the target word produced either with /d/ deletion or without. Again, the authors observed that the more proficient learners more often preferred the forms with /d/ deletion, suggesting that they had developed an awareness of this feature as being linked to certain regional varieties of

Spanish. In addition, the more advanced learners also started to become sensitive to other variables constraining the production of /d/ deletion, including amongst others speaker gender, in the sense that, just like native speakers, they associate /d/ deletion more often with male than female speakers.

5.2.5 First Language Accent Variation in Second Language Acquisition

Accent variation in language is omnipresent and hence if we examine the way in which learners acquire an L2, the study of how accent variation in the L1 impacts the learning process cannot be missing. Accent variation can be both social and regional in nature, the former depending on the socio-economic status of the speaker, the social context or register, and the latter on the speaker's regional background. As Thomas (2013) points out, previous research on accent variation mostly focused on production, though the number of perception studies is increasing. Several studies have demonstrated that L1 accent variation may impact the way in which learners perceive speech sounds in the L2. An example is the perception study by Chládková and Podlipsky (2011) on Czech listeners. In their study, two groups of L1 Czech listeners with different L1 accents, Bohemian Czech and Moravian Czech, were asked to map auditory stimuli containing Dutch vowels in a fixed consonantal frame (/hVb/) onto orthographic representations of Czech 'hVb' nonsense words. The Czech participants were naïve listeners of Dutch, meaning that they had not previously been exposed to Dutch. The results of this forced-choice identification task revealed that the Czech listeners indeed differed in the way they mapped the Dutch vowels onto Czech ones, depending on their regional L1 accent. As the authors note, this means that even small differences in L1 accents may have an effect on cross-language perceptual assimilation, such that the learning task for these two groups would also differ.

Similar findings have been reported for non-naïve listeners of the L2 who had been exposed to and were learners of the foreign language. For instance, Escudero et al. (2012) investigated L2 English vowel perception by L1 Dutch learners of English with either North Holland or East and West Flemish accents. In this study the results of a cross-language categorization task and an English identification task showed that in both tasks, North Holland listeners – unlike Flemish listeners – often mapped English /æ/ onto Dutch /ɑ/ (as in 'das', tie) and English /ɑ/ (as in 'darts'). This pattern could be explained by the acoustic differences in vowel realizations in North Holland and Flemish Dutch. Escudero and Williams (2012) addressed the same question for Peruvian Spanish and Iberian Spanish listeners of L2 Dutch, all living in the Netherlands at the time of the experiment, but with different proficiency levels in Dutch. The results of a perception experiment indicated that the Iberian Spanish listeners were better able at discriminating the Dutch /a-ɑ/ contrast, compared to the Peruvian Spanish listeners. Although both Iberian and Peruvian Spanish have only /a/, the acoustic properties of the vowels /a/ and /o/ in Iberian Spanish (higher F1 values) make them a better fit for Dutch /a-ɑ/ than the more closed qualities of these vowels in Peruvian Spanish.

Studies have also illustrated the effect of accent variation in the L1 on L2 production. An example of such a study is that by Turner (2022). In this study on the processing and production of the French /u/-/y/ contrast by L1 Standard Southern British English speakers, it was found that the participants' productions of the French /y/ vowel (as in 'vue', view) was more target-like, compared to their productions of French /u/ (as in 'vous', you). A cross-linguistic acoustic comparison revealed that the French /u/ vowel was acoustically more dissimilar to the English equivalent vowel /u/ than the French /y/ vowel. This is the result of extensive GOOSE-fronting in Southern Standard British English (Strycharczuk & Scobbie, 2017), which was the variety the participants spoke or were most familiar with. However, other production studies have shown more mixed results. For instance, we investigated the perception and production of L1 Standard Dutch and L2 English vowels by L1 Dutch speakers of East Flemish and Brabantine accents, in which vowels have different spectral and durational properties (Simon, Debaene & Van Herreweghe, 2015). The results of the production (picture-naming) tasks revealed that the participants' pronunciation of L1 Standard Dutch vowels differed between the two groups, as the result of their differing regional accents. However, no major differences could be observed between the two groups in their productions of L2 English vowels. In the paper, we argued that one explanation might be that the Dutch speakers' Standard Dutch vowels, shared between participant groups, rather than their regionally accented L1 vowels, influenced L2 English production. In a more recent study, Aksu (2022) found that Istanbul and Trabzon speakers of L1 Turkish produced Turkish /ʌ/ significantly different in their L1, but more similarly in L2 English. However, L2 English vowels that do not occur in Turkish, such as /ɒ/-/ɑː/ were realized differently, depending on the speakers' regional Turkish accents.

5.3 Concluding Remarks

In this section, we discussed whether research in sociophonetics can further our understanding of processes of phonological acquisition, and specifically, whether it can provide insight into the nature and acquisition of phonological representations in an L2. Traditionally, sociophonetic information was not considered relevant for theory building in phonology. More recently, however, awareness has grown that social and linguistic information are intertwined and invariably present in natural speech and are hence acquired *from the very beginning* of the acquisition process. This has led to the idea that any acquisition or learning model in which both types of information (linguistic and social) are processed and stored together is desirable. One such model that has been proposed is a hybrid exemplar-based model in which a layer of stable phonological knowledge, based on abstract phonological representations, is combined with a layer of fine (socio)phonetic detail that is updated as new exemplars are encountered in the acoustic input.

Given that previous studies on the acquisition of sociophonetic features have mostly been conducted on children acquiring their native language and on mobile speakers acquiring a new accent in their L1, the field of L2 sociophonetics is still relatively small. This is surprising, given that the acquisition of socio-indexical information in an L2 is part and parcel of the acquisition process, as learners need sensitivity to and knowledge of sociophonetic variables to navigate different kinds of social situations and interactions. Recent studies by Chappell and Kanwit (2022) and Solon and Kanwit (2022) have shown that L2 learners can pick up socio-indexical features in an L2, but that the extent to which they do depends on linguistic experience and L2 proficiency. While recency and frequency of exposure play an important role in L2 sociophonetic acquisition and 'full mastery' is said to be unattainable for L2 learners in the absence of these, it should be noted that the same may hold for L1 speaker-listeners. Native speakers of Dutch in the Netherlands, for instance, will lack sociophonetic knowledge about Belgian Dutch regional and social accents, unless they have received sufficient exposure to them. Besides amount of exposure, and as illustrated by Clopper and Bradlow (2009), the L1 exerts an influence on the perception of L2 sociophonetic information, as L2 listeners were shown to sometimes attend to cues which are relevant in their L2, but not in the L1 and vice versa ignored relevant L2 cues which play no socio-indexical role in their L1.

The extent to which sociophonetic variability affects intelligibility is another issue that has received little attention in research so far. From a number of recent studies, it emerges that regionally accented speech may not have a negative impact on the actual intelligibility, though more studies are needed to corroborate this finding (cf. Simon et al., in prep.). It would, however, be in line with earlier and older studies that have investigated the intelligibility of non-native accented speech by L1 listeners. In an oft-cited study on native listeners' judgements and understanding of Mandarin Chinese speakers' L2 English speech, Munro and Derwing (1995a) observed no strong correlation between accentedness (level of 'foreign accent') and intelligibility, in that even speakers who were judged to have a strong accent were highly intelligible (see also Munro & Derwing, 2020, where they provide retrospective commentary on their 1995a paper). Of course, the listeners in that study were listening to their L1, which – as noted before – is crucially different from listening in an L2.

In the previous sections, we have discussed how L2 learners have to build robust phonological representations (Section 3), while at the same time being flexible enough to deal with the large amount of phonetic variability present in speech (Section 4). We have seen that building this type of robust but flexible representations is a difficult task for L2 learners, who have already acquired a set of phonological representations for their L1. In Section 6, we take a look at the population of atypically developing language users, who are reported to differ from typically developing speakers in the formation of L1 phonological categories (Section 6.1). We then explore whether observations made about L1 phonological representations in clinical linguistics studies may also apply to (typically developing) adult L2 learners (Section 6.2).

6 Fuzzy and Overspecified Representations

6.1 Phonological Representations in Atypically Developing Language Users

The nature of phonological representations is also a research topic in clinical linguistics. Children or adults with atypical development in communication and/or reading and writing are reported to perform poorly on phonological awareness (PA) tasks such as phoneme deletion tasks (e.g. 'drop the first sound of the word *black*'), word learning tasks or non-word repetition tasks, all of which require language users to parse words into distinct and robust phonological units (Bishop & Snowling, 2004; Swan & Goswami, 1997). The low performance on PA tasks is often linked to a central phonological impairment (though see Pan & Chen, 2005 for evidence on the lack of universality of the role of PA), which would equally affect lexical retrieval (slower for impaired readers) and phonological memory (problems with perceiving or encoding speech sounds for temporary storage) (cf. Long et al., 2016). However, there does not seem to be consensus on the nature of the impairment – that is, where exactly do atypically developing language users differ from typically developing ones? A review of the literature on the topic reveals three main points of view.

First, many scholars have argued that the impairment is due to 'fuzzy' or 'low-quality' representations, meaning phonological representations which show overlap between phonemic categories (Claessen & Leitão, 2012). Such overlap would make it difficult for language users to establish robust grapheme-to-phoneme correspondences, inhibiting reading ability. Similarly, Maillart, Schelstraete and Hupet (2004) argue for 'underspecified' representations in children with atypical development. They conducted a French lexical decision task with seventy-five French-speaking children, of whom twenty-five were diagnosed with a developmental speech disorder, while the remaining fifty showed typical language development. The children were aged four to seven and matched for lexical age, based on their performance on a receptive vocabulary test. The results showed that both groups of children performed equally high on real words (i.e. they accepted them with more than 90 per cent accuracy), but that the atypically developing children had difficulty rejecting pseudo words which differed from real words through slight modifications, specifically through the addition or deletion of a segment in initial or final position. When larger modifications were made, affecting the number of syllables in the word, the atypically developing children were well able to reject the non-words. In addition, children's performance increased with receptive vocabulary level. The authors take the results to suggest that atypically developing children have more holistic, underspecified phonological representations, making them capable of detecting larger modifications, but not more subtle, segmental changes. The results further point towards a gradual refinement of phonological representations, as the size of the (receptive) lexicon increases, thereby confirming earlier studies on the relation between vocabulary growth and the development of phonological representations.

A second point of view, however, is advocated in a more recent study by Li et al. (2019). They set up an eye-tracking study with native speakers of English with a wide range of reading-related skills, as assessed through an extensive test battery. The participants were presented with unambiguous words (e.g. 'neck' [nɛk]) and words that had misleading coarticulation on the vowel and can be considered 'phonological competitors' (e.g. [nɛₖt], cross-spliced from 'neck' and 'net'). The results revealed a negative correlation between phonological skills, as assessed through reading-related tasks (amongst others a non-word repetition and phoneme deletion task), and mismatch negativity responses; in other words, individuals with lower phonological skills were more sensitive to sub-phonemic deviations compared to those with higher phonological skills. If these individuals' phonological representations had been underspecified, they would – quite to the contrary – be less distracted by sub-phonemic details. Therefore, the authors argue that the phonological representations in adults with low reading skills are over- rather than underspecified. This does not mean that typically developing listeners do not use allophones in perception. Mitterer, Reinisch and McQueen (2018) report on a series of three experiments on selective adaptation. Selective adaptation refers to the phenomenon where prolonged exposure to a specific linguistic stimulus (like a particular sound or word) causes a temporary change in the perception of similar stimuli (Eimas &

Corbit, 1973). They found that listeners only displayed selective adaptation if adaptors and test stimuli shared allophones. If they only shared context-independent phonemes (e.g. two different allophones of Dutch /l/), no selective adaptation was observed. The difference between typically and atypically developing listeners may thus lie in the type of sub-phonemic detail they attend to and in its relevance in the specific language they are listening to.

Finally, some scholars have argued that the phonological impairment may, in fact, be due to impaired access to phonological representations rather than to a deviant degree of specificity in the phonological representations themselves. In other words, the impairment would result from a processing issue rather than from a problem at the representational level. This argument is proposed by Long et al. (2016) in a study on children and adults with dyslexia, which the authors point out is part of a phonological impairment, rather than a cognitive deficit related to decoding written language. Participants performed a randomized forced-choice identification task with speech samples from two different areas, Ohio (the participants' residence) and North Carolina. The results revealed that, overall, children were outperformed by adults, but also and more crucially, that individuals with dyslexia performed significantly more poorly compared to participants with average reading abilities. In other words, both children and adults with dyslexia had not acquired socio-indexical features related to different dialects to the same extent. They also did not show a response bias for their own dialect: in the case of ambiguous stimuli, the dyslectic children and adults did not favour their own Ohio dialect as the response option, in contrast to the participants with average reading abilities. These findings are in line with earlier studies demonstrating that individuals with dyslexia are deficient in the extent to which they can adapt to multiple, unfamiliar talkers in their native language (Perrachione et al., 2011). Since the dyslectic adults in Long et al.'s (2016) study were, however, able to categorize talker dialects, the authors surmise that the phonological representations are actually intact (rather than under- or overspecified), but that access to these representations is impeded as the result of a less efficient working memory, which would also be responsible for difficulties with talker normalization. To date, research on the acquisition of socio-indexical speech features by children with atypical development seems relatively limited. An unpublished thesis by Laase (2015), however, seems to point in the same direction. This study examined whether children diagnosed with Williams syndrome, a genetic disorder that causes learning and cognitive disabilities, had acquired salient acoustic (vowel) properties of their native regional dialect of American English. The results revealed that participants in the clinical group acquired only some features of their regional variety in production: the children's vowel spaces were relatively idiosyncratic and contained only a selection of the typical regional accent features, compared to the typically developing children. The acquisition of socio-indexical language features thus appeared to be impeded in children with Williams syndrome.

6.2 Fuzzy Representations in Second Language Learners?

Although the causes of decreased PA in individuals with atypical language development are far from well understood, a question that arises is whether the low-quality or fuzzy representations argued by some to occur in atypical development may also emerge in L2 learners with typical development. This idea is somewhat appealing, as L2 learners' problems with perceiving and producing L2 contrasts that do not occur in the L1 may be due to either the lack of a phonemic split or to phonological representations whose boundaries are blurred and lack robustness. In 2022, the notion of fuzzy phonological representations in L2 learning was the topic of a special issue in *Bilingualism: Language and Cognition*, with a keynote by Bordag, Gor and Opitz (2022), seventeen commentaries by peers and an authors' response. In the same year (2022), *Frontiers in Communication* invited contributions to the research topic 'Fuzzy lexical representations in the non-native lexicon', leading to the online publication of one editorial and twelve research papers. While a comprehensive discussion of this whole body of research would obviously lead us too far, we briefly outline the main points here.

Bordag et al. (2022) introduce the Ontogenesis Model of L2 Lexical Representation (OM), which they argue is best described as 'a model of the non-native lexicon', which captures properties of L2 lexical units and seeks to map the development of L2 representations. A key idea of the model is that sometime along their developmental history (or 'ontogeny') representations may reach their 'optimum', meaning that they are 'properly encoded and fully specified' (185). The argument is that while L1 representations typically reach this optimum, lexical representations in the L2 typically do not reach this state but instead remain fuzzy, and move dynamically along the continuum from 'weak' to 'robust', sometimes coming closer to the optimum, sometimes moving further away from it, for instance during periods of little L2 exposure or use. The concept of 'fuzziness' is hence central to the model and defined as 'inexact or ambiguous encoding of different components or dimensions of the lexical representations that can be caused by several linguistic, cognitive, and learning-induced factors' (186).

In the OM, a lexical representation includes semantic, phonological and orthographic knowledge. In fully specified lexical representations, these three domains are well interconnected, facilitating lexical retrieval. In L2 representations, the connection may be looser. Each of the dimensions may start developing at a different point in time and may follow a different path in the acquisition process, with some reaching the optimum faster than others, which may be slower or never reach ultimate attainment.

In the large number of commentaries to this proposal, strong points as well as weaknesses of the model are discussed. Summarizing, the strength of the model lies in its attempt to provide a unified account of different dimensions of lexical representations, including phonological, orthographic and semantic properties, and that it includes a model for the development of these dimensions for L2 learners. However, the model faces a number of important challenges, identified in several commentaries. One issue is that the notions on which it crucially relies need to be more properly defined. What is the nature of fuzziness, exactly? Can it develop over time and does it lie in one feature, a whole syllable, or is it something more global (Darcy, 2022)? What exactly is the 'optimum' that representations need to reach (Ellis, 2022; Lemhöfer, 2022)? Additionally, and critically, the model at this point fails to formulate testable predictions. Escudero and Hayes-Harb (2022) argue that for the model to have explanatory power it needs to incorporate a model of the initial state – that is, what do the learners' representations look like at the start of L2 acquisition, what is the role of perception in mapping acoustic, orthographic and semantic input onto representations, and which stages are predicted in the development of representations towards the optimum? Nicol (2022), also in a peer commentary on Bordag et al.'s (2022) paper, further claims that the problem for advanced L2 learners may lie in the processing rather than in the representations. She (2022) argues that '[i]n order to convincingly argue in favor of fuzzy form representations in the L2 mental lexicon, it is essential to present converging evidence not just from comprehension tasks – where WM [working memory, our note] limitations may play a role – but also from production tasks' (231). The assumption here is that, if learners' productions deviate from the target forms in the same direction as predicted by perception data, the L2 forms differ from the L1 ones as the result of representational differences.

6.3 Concluding Remarks

In sum, research on atypically developing children and adults diagnosed with low reading abilities points in the direction of a general phonological impairment, which manifests itself as poorer performance on phonological awareness tasks, lexical retrieval tasks and tasks involving phonological memory. While much earlier research seemed to lay the cause of this impairment with 'fuzzy' or underspecified representations, other studies point towards a heightened sensitivity to sub-phonemic (and phonologically hence irrelevant) variation resulting from overspecified representations. However, research on the acquisition of socio-indexical features, such as regional dialect properties, suggests that individuals with low reading abilities may in fact have intact representations (as they are able to recognize regional accents), but have problems with processing, leading to a slower and less accurate recognition. This hypothesis is in line with earlier studies which have shown that atypical readers show poorer performance on talker normalization tasks – that is, have difficulty recognizing multiple talkers, presumably due to the higher processing costs involved in speech processing.

In L2 phonology, the idea of fuzzy representations has been proposed in the OM by Bordag et al. (2022), which aims to provide a unified account for how representations include different dimensions, including phonological, orthographic and semantic information. However, although the idea is appealing, it is clear that the concepts need to be defined in more detail and a more elaborate model of the initial state and developmental paths needs to be proposed, in order to formulate testable predictions. In addition, and in line with the literature on atypical development in child L1 learners, it remains difficult to tease apart processing difficulties from representational issues. Production studies complementing perception experiments may be needed to disentangle the two (Lemhöfer, 2022).

7 Assessing the Formation of Categories

7.1 Perception Studies as a Window into the Mental Lexicon

In Sections 3 to 5, we have discussed which aspects and properties, both linguistic and socio-indexical, need to be acquired by L2 learners and how these features may develop over time as a result of continued exposure to (variable) input and growing proficiency in the target language. Assuming that at some level of a language's phonology there is a layer of abstract phonological representations or categories (see Section 2.2 for Baese-Berk et al.'s 2022 definition), these representations gradually need to become more robust, with well-defined boundaries. At the same time, they need to be flexible and capable of shifting to accommodate for the variable acoustic input. In addition, sociophonetic knowledge in the form of socio-indexical features need to be attached to these categories in a surface layer containing fine phonetic detail. A crucial question in the field of L2 phonology is then how it can be established whether learning has taken place, and more specifically, whether categories have been formed. This general question can be split up into three more specific ones:

1) How do we know whether robust representations have been formed in the L2?
2) How do we know whether flexible representations have been formed in the L2?
3) How do we know whether socio-indexical features of the L2 have been acquired?

To address question (1) about the formation of robust categories in L2 learners, researchers have typically used perception studies to gain insight into the emergence of phonological categories in L2 learners, as these are thought to offer a better window into learners' grammar than production studies, in which the output may reflect articulatory constraints rather than internal structure or representations (e.g. articulatory difficulty to produce interdental friction in English /θ/). Often used tasks in experimental perception studies include identification and discrimination tasks. In identification tasks, listeners are presented with auditory stimuli and are asked to identify the target sounds by clicking on one of several visual representations on the screen. For instance, they hear the English word 'but' [bʌt] and are presented with a selection of orthographic forms, including, for instance, 'bet', 'bat', 'bit', 'boot' and 'but', from which they are asked to pick one. The results of L2 identification tasks provide us with information on how L2 listeners map the acoustic input of target sounds onto L2 phonemic categories and can hence provide insight into the presence or absence of L2 representations. A myriad of studies on different languages have used L2 identification tasks to get insight into L2 learners' development (see Nagle and Baese-Berk, 2022 for a discussion of this task). In addition, studies have used cross-language categorization tasks in which listeners are asked to map target L2 sounds onto L1 categories on the screen. The aim of these tasks is to get a better understanding of the perceptual mappings and correspondences between the L1 and the L2. Lexical decision tasks, in which listeners are presented with an auditory stimulus and have to judge whether the stimulus is a real word (e.g. 'cave') or a non-word (e.g. 'tave'), are similar to identification tasks, in that learners need to access their knowledge about L2 phonological categories in order to reach a decision.

Discrimination tasks reveal whether listeners are able to perceive differences and similarities between L2 sounds. One commonly used discrimination task is the AXB task, in which listeners hear a sequence of three auditory stimuli and are asked to indicate whether sound 'X' is most similar to sound 'A' or 'B'. (Variants have been proposed, such as the XAB and the ABX tasks, in which the target stimulus comes at, respectively, the very beginning or the very end). Oddity tasks also exist in different forms. In a four-interval-oddity task, listeners hear four sounds in a row and are asked to press a button to indicate which one of these is deviant or, in other words, 'sounds different from the others'. Often, the auditory stimuli – in both types of tasks – are not acoustically identical; instead they are different realizations by the same speaker or tokens produced by different speakers. When this is the case, and there is a sufficiently long interstimulus interval (1,000–2,000 milliseconds), these tasks are argued to tap phonological knowledge, as learners are not able to just rely on a comparison between sounds at the auditory level (Mora, 2007).

The second question is how it can be established whether learners have built representations which are flexible enough to cope with phonetic variation in the acoustic input. In Section 4.2, we reviewed previous studies on perceptual adaptation to accented speech. Often, these studies make use of lexical decision tasks, preceded by a familiarization phase, in which listeners are exposed to unfamiliar phonetic realizations or unfamiliar boundaries. A typical example of the latter would be to familiarize listeners with a VOT contrast that doesn't exist in their L1, such as presenting a three-way VOT contrast (e.g. Thai) to listeners of English, which has only a two-way contrast between short-lag and long-lag aspirated stops. These studies provide us with information on learners' ability to shift phonemic boundaries after exposure to accented speech. Insightful as these studies are, they do not provide us with information on the flexibility of phonological representations of L2 listeners when they are exposed to, for instance, accented speech. The question remains unanswered whether in those cases, listeners need to *adapt* their perception or whether their category boundaries need to be flexible enough to deal with this kind of variation from the start.

While perceptual adaptation studies are grounded in the psycholinguistic research tradition, the perception of accented speech is often couched in intelligibility research, which has a history in research on L2 acquisition. With the shifting focus in L2 pronunciation teaching – away from native speaker models and towards intelligibility as a more feasible or desirable pronunciation goal – intelligibility research has been on the rise in the past decades. While early studies on intelligibility (see Section 4.5) were mostly concerned with the extent to which L2 speakers' pronunciation was intelligible to native listeners, more recently, intelligibility research has moved away from being centered around native speaker-listener models. The idea that intelligibility depends not only on the speakers and their speech, but is equally determined by listeners has gained ground. For instance, the listener's L1, their familiarity with the speaker's language or accent and the extent of contact the listener has with the language will all play a role in the extent to which a speaker will be comprehensible or intelligible (Simon et al., 2022). A study by

Winke, Gass and Myford (2013) showed that language test-raters who had studied Spanish or Chinese as a foreign language were significantly more lenient in their comprehensibility ratings of, respectively, Spanish- and Chinese-accented English speech samples (see also, e.g., Lippi-Green, 1994 on the impact of listeners' goodwill in communicative success). A number of studies have examined to what extent regional and/or non-native speech is intelligible to L2 learners (see Section 5.2.3). Typically, such intelligibility tasks involve transcription of sentences (sometimes nonsensical, to reduce predictability effects based on semantic context) or individual words (e.g. fill-in-the-blank task). These tasks provide evidence for how well L2 listeners deal with non-native speech in non-optimal conditions (see, e.g., Verbeke & Simon, 2023a, on the intelligibility of different native and non-native varieties of English). As recently discussed by Baese-Berk et al. (2023), however, it is unclear to what extent intelligibility research can actually help us assess whether perceptual acquisition has taken place. In fact, the authors argue that intelligibility data can typically not provide information on the *causes* of listening challenges and hence tell us little about the L2 learners' phonological representations. In order to take that step, different tasks are needed in which the stimuli are controlled and which test the intelligibility of words differing in specific alternating target segments.

The third question just formulated is how we can assess whether learners have acquired socio-indexical features in the L2. It is in this respect useful to consider the distinction made in the literature between conscious knowledge of socio-indexical features and subconscious perception of those features (Schmidt, 1990). Montgomery and Moore (2018) investigated the former in L1 English listeners, using a self-developed Salient Language In Context (SLIC) tool that allows participants to listen to speech samples in different accents while clicking a button whenever they notice a social feature that is particularly salient to them. This behavioural procedure, in which listeners can also review their clicks and explain why certain features were notable, explicitly addresses L1 listeners' ability to notice sociophonetic features in different accents. As noted in Section 5.2.3, to date few studies have investigated the acquisition of sociophonetic features by L2 learners. In a recent set of studies Dailey (2024) explored L1 and L2 French listeners' perception of sociophonetic cues to formal and informal registers in Metropolitan French. Specifically, the studies focus on optional liaison in phrases like 'plats [z] italiens' ('Italian dishes'), associated with formal register, and post-obstruent liquid deletion in words like 'table' [tab] ('table'), typical for informal, everyday speech. Using a matched-guise technique, Dailey found that, unlike the L1 listeners, the L2 listeners only perceived speech containing liaison as more or less formal when they explicitly noticed the sociophonetic feature. Liquid deletion, by contrast, was associated with informal, everyday speech by L1 and L2 listeners even when they did not consciously notice the feature. Dailey (2024) argues that the liquid deletion results suggest that the L2 listeners were able to acquire the social meaning of this feature, possibly helped by the fact that liquid deletion is a reduction phenomenon, which is cross-linguistically typical of casual speech. In order to explain the absence of a liaison effect and the minimal noticing of optional liaison displayed by the L2 listeners, Dailey refers to the stereotypical character of optional liaison in French. The L1 French listeners must have picked up the feature as part of being raised in a French educational and cultural context, in which this feature is associated with formal speech produced by prestigious speakers with upper-class professions. Even the highly advanced L2 listeners remained unfamiliar with this stereotype and did not make social inferences from the feature.

To conclude, the development of robust phonological representations in L2 learners can be investigated through perception tasks, such as identification, categorization or discrimination tasks, which provide insight into the phonemic or phonetic categories formed by the learners. Whether L2 learners' phonological representations are flexible enough to deal with phonetic variability due to, for instance, regional accents, is typically examined though intelligibility tasks, such as transcription tasks involving accented speech fragments, or in lexical decision tasks, in which a familiarization phase is followed by a test phase. Studies examining the acquisition of socio-indexical features by L2 learners are not abundant yet, but use metalinguistic noticing tasks or matched-guise techniques. In a hybrid model of phonological representations, in which sociophonetic features are associated with abstract phonemic categories, the acquisition of social meaning is part of the phonological acquisition process. If L2 listeners display associations of particular phonetic cues with social features, such as register or regional background, this means that they have acquired at least part of the phonological representation.

7.2 The Role of Production Studies

So far, all the evidence we have cited for category formation comes from perception studies, as these are generally assumed to offer a more direct window onto learners' mental representations compared to production studies. The reason is that in production tasks, articulatory constraints may lead to discrepancies between the speech sounds speakers aim to produce and their actual pronunciations. A typical example in L2 English research is the production of (inter)dental fricatives (e.g. onset consonants in 'think' /θ/ and 'they' /ð/), which are known to pose articulatory challenges to L2 learners. Even when L2 learners have developed robust mental representations for these speech sounds and strive to pronounce the sounds in line with these representations, they may fail to produce appropriate friction at the dental place of articulation, if the combination of these articulatory gestures is unfamiliar to them from their L1 (as would be the case in, e.g., Dutch, German and French). Perception studies, by contrast, can provide us directly with information on which cues are detected by the listener in the acoustic input and how these cues are mapped onto phonological representations (Archibald, 2023).

However, this does not mean that production data cannot reveal anything about the acquisition of phonological representations. A recent study by Turner (2024), for instance, examines the effect of a residence abroad in a French-speaking country on the acquisition of the French sounds /u/ (as in 'vous', you) and /y/ (as in 'vue', view) by L1 speakers of English, which lacks this vowel contrast. In the study, categorical changes in production are taken to reflect phonological acquisition, while gradient changes reflect changes in phonetic properties of the sounds in question. Specifically, if the learners increasingly produce what for them is a /u/ vowel in French /u/ items and an /y/ vowel in French /y/ items, this is taken as evidence for phonological acquisition. By contrast, gradient, phonetic acquisition is said to take place if the learners' phonologically accurate /u/ and /y/ vowels become acoustically more target-like during the residence abroad (Turner, 2024). The results of the production study revealed a significant phonetic development in French /y/, as well as a developing phonological representation for French /u/ over the residence abroad. Different input factors, such as quantity and quality of input over the stay abroad, amount of previous naturalistic exposure and length of time learning French, had a differential impact on L2 development. For instance, the quantity and quality of input during the residence abroad more strongly determined phonological compared to phonetic development.

In addition, many studies have addressed the relationship between L2 speech perception and L2 speech production (see Nagle & Baese-Berk, 2022 for a comprehensive overview and discussion). If a tight link between the two modalities is assumed, this implies that L2 production would develop hand in hand with L2 perception, meaning that both perception and production studies would be able to provide us with evidence of category formation. However, while it is clear that there is a link between perception and production in L2 learners, the nature of this link is still in need of further investigation. Previous studies have, for instance, demonstrated that L2 learners may be able to produce L2 sounds in a target-like manner without being able to reliably distinguish between them in perception. An often-cited study is the research by Sheldon and Strange (1982), who demonstrated that some L1 Japanese learners of English were able to produce English /r/ and /l/ before being able to accurately perceive these speech sounds, at least in pre-vocalic consonant clusters. In addition, asking participants to produce words during L2 speech sound learning (i.e. learning at the sub-lexical level) has been shown to have a disruptive rather than facilitatory effect on perceptual learning (Baese-Berk, Kapnoula & Samuel, 2024). These findings have led some scholars to propose separate developmental routes for perceptual and production representations. While a review of studies on the perception–production link would lead us too far afield, the general picture that emerges is that the two modalities may be more or less closely linked to one another at different levels of representation (cf. also Baese-Berk et al., 2024).

In the following sections, we single out two types of production studies that might be helpful in exploring the extent to which production studies can provide us with information on the acquisition of mental representations: phonetic convergence studies and articulatory phonetics studies.

7.2.1 Phonetic Convergence

One type of production studies that is interesting in light of the question whether learners have acquired L2 categories are studies on phonetic convergence, also referred to as phonetic alignment or speech accommodation. In these studies, it is investigated to what extent speakers adopt features of the speech of their interlocutor. In Section 5.2.2, we discussed research in the field of second dialect acquisition, which investigates to what extent mobile speakers adapt their L1 accent to that spoken in the area to which they have moved or to the speakers of the community to which they want to belong. In line with general intuitions about people changing their accents when spending a long time in a different dialect region, there is ample scientific evidence that speakers indeed tend to align their speech to that of their interlocutors. This has been shown in studies examining phonetic convergence in interactional settings (e.g. Pardo et al., 2012 on phonetic convergence in American college roommates) as well as in experimental contexts (e.g. Delvaux & Socquet, 2007 on phonetic convergence/imitation to Belgian French accents presented over loudspeakers). An example of a task used in experimental studies is the shadowing task, in which participants are asked to repeat spoken utterances as fast as possible. For instance, Mitterer and Müsseler (2013) found that the L1 German listeners adapted their production in the direction of different German accents in the stimuli they were asked to repeat.

However, phonetic convergence or imitation studies have also revealed a number of restrictions to phonetic convergence, referred to by Goldrick and

Cole (2023) as the non-uniformity of phonetic convergence. First, there are linguistic restrictions, in that speakers seem to pick certain features which they adapt to those of their interlocutors, while leaving other features unchanged. One study that is particularly relevant in this respect is that by Nielsen (2011), who examined phonetic imitation of unfamiliar VOT patterns by L1 American English speakers. The results of two experiments revealed that speakers imitated overlong, extended VOTs in English /t/ and generalized this to new /t/ tokens as well as to /p/ tokens. However, target speech with reduced VOT values was not imitated. An explanation can be found in the phonological system of English: whereas phonetically overlong VOTs do not interfere with another phonemic category (i.e. a strongly aspirated [tʰ] will still be categorized as /t/), reduced VOT values in voiceless plosives may cause merger with the phonemic category of voiced plosives, which in English are typically produced with a short-lag VOT (i.e. a short lag [t] may be categorized as /d/).

Secondly, phonetic convergence is not only linguistically determined, but also socially mediated. For instance, a recent study by Clopper and Dossey (2020) investigated phonetic convergence towards Southern American English by non-Southern speakers. The participants in their study displayed clear phonetic convergence in a shadowing task ('repeat what the speaker says') and even more so in an imitation task ('imitate what the speaker says') in terms of word duration and back vowel fronting, but not in monophthongization of /aɪ/. The absence of convergence to /aɪ/ monophthongization is explained by the authors in relation to the social meaning attached to this feature, as it is a highly stereotyped feature of Southern American English. A study by Babel (2012) similarly provides proof of a non-uniform treatment of features in a shadowing task, in which some vowels but not others were articulated in the direction of the model talkers, both speakers of standard Californian English. In one condition, participants saw a picture of a Black speaker and a White speaker on the screen as visual prompts. An analysis of the participants' productions revealed that participants who rated the speaker higher on an attractiveness scale showed stronger phonetic convergence than others. The extent of phonetic convergence will crucially hinge on the question whether speakers identify with their interlocutors and have a (subconscious or conscious) wish to become an in-group member of the (speech) community.

To conclude, there is sufficient evidence to argue that phonetic convergence studies can provide us with information on speakers' phonological representations. The linguistic restrictions on phonetic convergence indicate that it is a process that is phonologically informed: as shown by Nielsen's (2011) study, phonetic convergence does not emerge if speakers know that a relevant phonemic contrast may be blurred or merged, which means that the occurrence or absence of phonetic convergence may give us insight into the phonological knowledge of the speakers. Moreover, phonetic convergence is informed by speakers' knowledge and sensitivity to socio-indexical features of language. If these features are stored as an integral part of phonological categories, as argued in hybrid models of phonological representations (see Section 5.2.2), this means that phonetic convergence studies can provide us with information on which socio-indexical features have been acquired by the speakers.

Phonetic convergence studies therefore also seem to be promising for the development of our knowledge on phonological representations in L2 learners. To date, relatively little research has been carried out on phonetic convergence in L2 speakers (but see recent work by Gnevsheva et al., 2021 and Jiang & Kennison, 2022). In Gnevsheva et al.'s (2021) study L1 Australian and American as well as Russian L2 learners of English performed a single-word shadowing task with an Australian and American talker. The results showed that overall the L2 speakers showed convergence on more features (F1 and F2 of more vowels) than the L1 speakers, which the authors attribute to the more malleable nature of the L2 learners' phonological representations. However, more work in this area is clearly needed to further explore phonetic convergence to linguistic and socio-indexical features in an L2 (cf. Kwon, MacLeod & Nielsen, 2024).

7.2.2 Articulatory Phonetics

A second set of production studies that may throw light on L2 learners' phonological categories are articulatory phonetics studies. In the field of linguistics, articulation itself was long considered as the topmost surface level of speech production and as such furthest removed from deeper phonological knowledge. In traditional phonological theory, phonological representations were considered to be abstract, in the sense that they do not have direct acoustic or articulatory correlates (Pierrehumbert, 2016). In fact, as noted earlier in this Element, articulatory restrictions were viewed as an obstacle to understanding phonological organization, as these may cause changes between the underlying forms and the produced forms. A theory that challenged this idea is the motor theory of speech perception, developed in the field of cognitive psychology by Liberman and colleagues (Liberman & Mattingly, 1985). The central premise of the model is that speech perception takes place via articulatory gestures, in the sense that when listeners perceive speech forms, they do not mainly rely on acoustic cues, but rather track the articulatory gestures of the speech organs in the vocal tract. For instance, when hearing a [b], listeners will track the constriction in the oral cavity formed by the lips, also when only the auditory signal is available (i.e. in the absence of visual cues showing the closed lips of the speaker).

Around the same time, Browman and Goldstein (1986, 1992) developed an articulatory model of phonology, in which articulatory gestures are the basic, invariable units of speech. In articulatory phonology, gestures are defined as 'abstract characterizations of articulatory events' (Browman & Goldstein, 1992: 155). These gestures can overlap, accounting for coarticulation phenomena in speech.

Arguments for and against the role of articulatory gestures in speech perception and the extent to which listeners access these gestures in perception have been provided in older as well as more recent publications (e.g. special issue in *Phonetica*, edited by Diehl, 1992; Tilsen, 2016). Important for the present Element on L2 phonology is that several current phonological models now assume rich representations, including information on the articulatory gestures associated or correlating with the target sounds in question. The question relevant to us now is whether data on articulatory gestures can provide insight into phonological development and representations of L2 learners. One influential speech learning model, PAM (Best, 1995), and its application for L2 learners, PAM-L2 (Best & Tyler, 2007) is couched in the tradition of direct-realist models of speech perception. The central tenet of such models is the (philosophical) idea that the perceiver must perceive the world directly, without mediation via a representative – that is, perceptual knowledge is acquired from the speech signal available to the perceiver (Best, 1995). In terms of speech perception, both motor theory and direct realist models assume the perceptual primitives to be articulatory gestures (the neuromotor commands, or the intended gestures in motor theory vs. the actual gestures in direct realist models). In cross-language speech perception, listeners perceive L2 speech in terms of the extent to which the articulatory gestures (location of constrictions and active articulators used) are similar to or different from the ones used for native L1 sounds. Non-native segments can then be (i) assimilated to a native category, (ii) perceived as a speech-like gestural constellation, but not assimilated to a native category, or (iii) perceived as non-speech – that is, not assimilated to speech sounds at all. Different predictions have been made for the perception of L2 contrasts (as opposed to L2 segments) (Best, 1995).

Much research testing the mapping of L2 speech sounds onto L1 categories predicted by PAM and PAM-L2 has used tasks in which listeners are asked to categorize L2 sounds as the closest L1 sounds or to discriminate between L2 sound contrasts. These studies typically include detailed acoustic measurements of the consonants or vowels produced in the stimuli (for an example of a recent study, see Lu & Ota, 2023). However, if listeners effectively perceive articulatory gestures, as assumed by the direct realist PAM, then detailed and accurate measurements of articulatory movements of the speech organs should, in fact, be preferred over acoustic measures of the speech sounds. Today, such measurements are possible with techniques such as electromagnetic articulography (EMA), which are used in specialized speech labs (see Rebernik et al., 2021 for a review paper on data collection practices using EMA). As a result, it is likely that in the future more studies testing predictions of models like PAM(-L2) will rely on articulatory rather than acoustic measurements and that more articulatory corpora, such as the Edinburgh Speech Production Facility DoubleTalk corpus (Scobbie et al., 2013), aligning audio with transcriptions and electromagnetic articulation data will be developed.

8 Avenues for Future Research: How to Advance the Field of Second Language Phonology?

In this section we put forward potential new avenues in L2 phonology research. We focus on two methodological opportunities, the use of natural and spontaneous speech in L2 research and the collection of large data sets through the use of online experiments (Section 8.1). In Section 8.2 we discuss a major challenge for research on L2 phonology, which is the incorporation of sociophonetic variation in the field. More specifically, we address the question of how to integrate the acquisition of socio-indexical information in models of L2 phonological acquisition.

8.1 Methodological Opportunities

8.1.1 Spontaneous Speech and Second Language Phonology Research

There is a trend in speech research these days to advocate the use of spontaneous data, which would enhance the ecological validity of studies on the perception and production of speech sounds. Ecological validity is defined by Kihlstrom (2021: 466) as 'the extent to which experimental findings can generalize to the "real world" situation that a researcher wishes to understand' (cf. also Verbeke, 2024 for a discussion on ecological validity in language and speech research). The question relevant to us in this Element is whether the use of spontaneous speech in L2 experiments will further our understanding of how L2 phonology is acquired. In other words, do experiments that use spontaneous speech have a good or even better potential of pushing the field of L2 phonology forward? In a recent Cambridge Element in Phonetics devoted entirely to the topic of spontaneous speech, Tucker and Mukai (2023) emphasize investigating spontaneous speech, pointing out that it is a central part of the wide range of speech types that speakers and listeners use: 'If the goal is to understand communication from the perspective of ecological validity (i.e., a sample that reflects actual speaker and listener experience), then it is important to understand how this range of speech types impacts speech production and perception' (2). The authors grant that it is difficult to determine the boundaries of what can be called spontaneous speech, because there are multiple dimensions to speech types: a careful-to-casual dimension, a fast-to-slow dimension and a reduced-to-unreduced dimension. As a working definition of spontaneous speech, they propose the following: 'Spontaneous speech is speech produced by a speaker in an informal, dynamic, unrehearsed, casual manner' (5).

As spontaneous speech is much more prevalent in everyday communication than formal, rehearsed and planned speech, it is clear that it should also be the object of investigation in research on L2 phonology. Studies in this field have often opted for the use of highly controlled laboratory speech, both for the study of L2 production and for L2 perception experiments. The advantages of this type of speech in these studies are obvious: the quality of the acoustic signal is high (background noise is absent) and – even more importantly – the produced speech can be controlled in several respects. Depending on the type of task, it is possible to monitor speech rate through instructions or by setting time limits, or to control the phonetic context of target segments. For instance, numerous L2 perception experiments on vowel acquisition have used stimuli in which vowels are included in fixed consonantal frames (such as 'hVd' and 'bVt') (e.g. Escudero et al., 2012). These studies are able to answer questions about how the vowels are perceived, without different consonantal contexts biasing the results. The disadvantage of such controlled stimuli lies, of course, precisely in their controlled nature: speakers do not normally produce vowels in these consonantal frames at the same speech rate, and listeners are not normally exposed to such forms. This does not need to be problematic, when the researcher's goal is to gain insight into mechanisms underlying speech perception, or when the research question is of a theoretical nature and the main goal of the study is to test, for instance, predictions made by different speech perception models (see, e.g., Chang, 2019 for a comparison of, e.g., PAM-L2 and SLM-r). If that is the case, there is great value in using more controlled laboratory data for perception experiments.

Using highly controlled speech may become problematic when the research question itself pertains to the acquisition of aspects of spontaneous speech in an L2. A well-known property of spontaneous speech is that it is subject to reduction processes which may be absent or at least less strongly present in formal, rehearsed speech. English, for instance, is well known for vowel reduction processes, causing words like 'family' to be pronounced as [fæm.li] or 'suppose' as [spəʊz], but such processes can be found in many languages. In a recent study, we aimed to answer the question to what extent phonetic reduction in several accents of English affects the perception and the intelligibility for L2 listeners with different native languages. Specifically, we investigated whether L1 English listeners and L2 listeners with either Dutch or Spanish as their native language differ in the extent to which reduced forms in different accents of English are intelligible to them. While vowel reduction is common in Dutch, it occurs to a far lesser extent in Spanish, which also lacks a schwa in its inventory. In order to assess the intelligibility of reduced and unreduced forms in context, participants performed a transcription task in which the target stimuli occurred in sentence-long utterances. These audio fragments were excised from longer broadcast interviews or talk shows, which were all publicly available online. In line with previous research (e.g. Ernestus & Baayen, 2007) and our hypothesis, reduced words were recognized less accurately compared to unreduced words, and L2 listeners had relatively more difficulty with reduced words than L1 listeners (see Figure 4). In contrast to what we had predicted, the L2 Spanish listeners did not have more trouble understanding reduced forms, suggesting that the presence of similar reduction processes in Dutch and English did not create an advantage for the Dutch listeners.

Because the target words were embedded in a semantic context which might have facilitated recognition, we set up a follow-up experiment consisting of a lexical decision task with the same stimuli in which we measured participants'

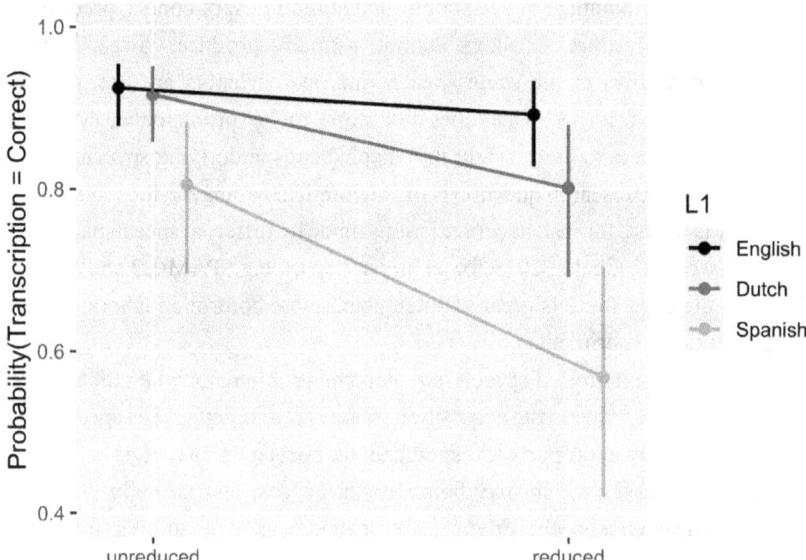

Figure 4 Effect display of two-way interaction between listener group and reduction condition (Verbeke, Mitterer & Simon, 2025).

reaction times. For that purpose, we needed to create non-words. In order for these non-words to sound as authentic as possible, we excised syllables from spontaneous words and merged them together. For instance, the non-word *submantic* (*/səbˈmæn.tɪk/) was created from *submerge* (/səbˈmɜːdʒ/) and *romantic* (/rəˈmæn.tɪk/). Results revealed that listeners needed more time to recognize reduced target words as real words compared to unreduced forms. Again, there was no difference between Spanish and Dutch listeners in terms of the effect of reduction: both groups were slowed down to a similar degree. The study provides insights into the role of phonetic reduction in the intelligibility of spontaneous speech by L2 listeners. Methodologically, it provides an example of a study that walks the line between using maximally spontaneous speech in perception experiments, and keeping control over the context and task. Although we decided to use authentic data from talk shows, the stimuli could not be randomly selected. In fact, they had to be carefully selected, so that we kept control over variables such as sentence duration, number of syllables, speaking rate, predictability of the target word within the sentence context (checked using a cloze task) and signal-to-noise ratios. As a result, the selection of these authentic stimuli was time-consuming.

One important implication of our decision to use authentic, spontaneous speech from talk shows is that it was impossible to include reduced and unreduced forms of the same words in the experiments, as these could simply not be found for the same speakers of the different accents. Arguably, it may be possible to collect such data in a laboratory setting, in which case speakers would be asked to produce sentences containing reduced and unreduced variants of the same word. In Xu's (2010) forum piece in *Journal of Phonetics*, several myths about lab speech are debunked, such as that lab speech is slow and careful, clear and articulate. As Xu argues, participants in the lab seem to have little difficulty following instructions about, for instance, the level of formality they are to use, and so it may be possible to elicit relatively spontaneous sounding stimuli differing in presence or absence of reduction, though these may lack a certain authenticity (cf. also Wagner, Trouvain & Zimmerer, 2015 on stylistic diversity in speech research).

Besides studies that specifically focus on the acquisition of properties of spontaneous speech, such as reduction, another type of L2 research for which spontaneous speech may be preferred over highly controlled speech is sociophonetic research, discussed in Section 3. In L2 sociophonetic studies, which, as we have argued, may contribute to our understanding of L2 phonological acquisition, we are interested in whether and how L2 learners acquire socio-indexical features of L2 accents. As the production of socio-indexical features is context-sensitive (e.g. more features in informal speech with members of the same community), the use of authentic, spontaneous speech in this field seems mandatory.

However, in a recent paper by van de Velde et al. (2022), the authors argue that in sociolinguistic research spontaneous speech has recently lost some of its previously unassailable status. Traditionally, variationist linguists greatly valued the study of speech data gathered in authentic communicative contexts. Some downsides of using authentic speech are, however, that variables are unequally distributed in speech samples (referred to as the frequency problem), that specific combinations occur infrequently (the co-occurrence problem) and that groups of speakers show different patterns of variation (the interaction problem) (van de Velde & van Hout, 2000). Given that experimental designs do not run into the same problems, van de Velde et al. (2022) advocate an approach which they call 'laboratory sociolinguistics', characterized as 'a branch of variationist sociolinguistics that makes use of laboratory techniques and quantitative research methods' (563). Recent studies examining the acquisition of sociophonetic variables in an L2 or in a second dialect using lab data produced with different degrees of spontaneity include Montgomery and Moore (2018), Vriesendorp (2021) and Dailey (2024).

In sum, we argue that L2 speech research would benefit from the inclusion of spontaneous speech data, especially when the research questions revolve around the acquisition of aspects of spontaneous speech, such as reductions or assimilation processes, or in L2 sociophonetic studies.

We agree with Tucker and Mukai (2023: 30) that studying speech perception using spontaneous speech is challenging and therefore argue that spontaneous speech should complement rather than replace more traditional lab speech or lab perception experiments. We discussed the feasibility of incorporating natural data in L2 perception experiments, pointing out that a balance needs to be found between using maximally spontaneous speech and keeping control over data to make sure that research questions can be answered.

8.1.2 Remote Data Collection and Crowdsourcing in Second Language Phonology

As a result of increased worldwide internet access and stimulated by the Covid-19 pandemic in 2019 and the following years, during which in-person testing was impossible, more and more L2 speech researchers are starting to explore remote data collection. This method entails that participants no longer come to the speech or experimental lab, or – vice versa – that the experimenter no longer visits participants at home or in other settings such as schools. Instead, the experiment is run fully online, with little or no personal contact between the researcher and the participant. Often, remote data collection is combined with the use of online crowdsourcing platforms such as Prolific (www.prolific.com) and Amazon Mechanical Turk (www.mturk.com). Pros and cons of remote data collection using online participant recruitment are being explored in specialist courses and discussed in recent papers and we refer the reader to these sources for more extensive discussions. (For an overview, see, e.g., Kenny Smith's materials available at Online Experiments for Language Scientists | Academic year 2023–2024 (kennysmithed.github.io) and Catanzariti (2022) on ethical issues in the use of crowdsourcing platforms.) However, we briefly discuss two implications of remote data collection that are particularly relevant for L2 phonology research, viz. the accessibility to different populations and the opportunity to collect large data sets in an incredibly small amount of time.

First, remote data collection via crowdsourcing platforms allows the researcher to reach specific linguistic populations. Although the participant pool available through online recruitment platforms is also restricted and less diverse than researchers may wish (e.g. mostly young, educated, un- or under-employed participate, Stewart, Chandler & Paolacci 2017), it is possible to pre-screen and select participants on the basis of L1 background. This is highly valuable for certain types of perception experiments, as it means that researchers can get insight into the role of different L1s on L2 perception (Verbeke et al., 2025). Without the use of these platforms, researchers in need of participants with a variety of L1s need to get in touch with local institutions, often universities, to announce and facilitate participant recruitment.

Secondly, running experiments online is much faster than in-person data collection in the lab or live at another location (e.g. a school) and a larger population can be reached. As a result, it is possible to collect much larger data sets in a shorter amount of time. This opportunity aligns well with the general trend in linguistic research to use more data per study and with the rise of 'big data', defined by Cohn and Renwick as 'a dataset that is too large and complex to be analysed by hand; instead such datasets require automated or computational tools like visualization, summary, statistical modelling for analysis' (Cohn & Renwick, 2019: 1). The authors note that naturalistic corpora are perhaps the most common type of large data sets, but that the data sets may also contain psycholinguistic data or laboratory speech. In the field of socio-phonetics, there is a trend towards using big data, as noted by Kendall and Fridland (2021):

> In addition, and perhaps crucial to the continuing development of the field's import more largely, the move from manual and typically small-scale data to more automated 'big data' approaches has benefits for advancing the study of

sound change, speech and identity, and other sociophonetic pursuits, not only because more data tends to make for better data, but because larger datasets often just offer us different insights. (189)

The authors refer to Gunter et al.'s (2020) study on /str/ retraction based on the Corpus of Regional African American Languages, and note that such a corpus, based on a large number of speakers, is necessary to get insight into the amount of variation and spread of features in different speaker groups (see also Breitbarth et al., 2023 with a special issue on big data in research on language variation and change). The same trend will trickle down in L2 sociophonetic studies, be it at a slower pace, because it is easier to collect large spoken data sets of L1 speech than of L2 speech. However, as noted by Gnevsheva (2022), with more researchers sharing data online, the same trend towards big data will eventually be observed in L2 research.

While the advantages of remote data collection are obvious, there are also undeniable downsides, including the low level of control of the participants' background information or context in which the experiments are run (e.g. background noise, level of concentration). In an ongoing study (De Haes et al., in prep.), we examine the sociophonetic knowledge in L1 listeners of French in Ile de France. In an accent verification task with French listeners recruited through Prolific, a condition for participation was that the participants had spent most of their childhood in the Ile de France region. This condition was explicitly mentioned on the screen at the start of the experiment and participants were instructed to only continue if they met this criterion. After completion of the task, participants were asked to indicate in which region they had spent most of their childhood, with the explicit mention that their answer would not affect payment. The results showed that of the fifty-nine participants who did the experiment and were paid through Prolific, twenty-three (39 per cent) claimed to meet the criterion of coming from the Ile de France region before the experiment, but reported to come from a different region in France (e.g. Provence in southern France) after the experiment. Observations like this stress the importance of incorporating checks on background information, especially when using crowdsourcing platforms, in which financial compensation is known to be the driving force for participation. (See Rodd, 2024 for a list of recommendations for ensuring data quality when running online experiments.)

It is clear that the trend towards the collection of large data sets through the use of crowdsourcing via participant recruitment platforms is also emerging in L2 speech research. Remote data collection has especially been used for perception studies, but new methods to collect production data are also currently being investigated (see Flege, 2021 on methods to elicit L2 production data, some of which can be used for internet data collection). In the coming years, more researchers will share their experiences with remote data collection and large data sets (cf., e.g., the Call for Papers for a special issue in *Laboratory Phonology*, entitled 'Distanced data collection: Remote data collection and online experimentation'). As our joint experience with and expertise in the methodology grows, researchers will be able to make informed decisions about the contexts in which large remote data collection is viable as well as those contexts in which it is preferable to resort to smaller-scale in-person experiments.

8.2 Theoretical Challenge: The Second Language as a Linguistic and Social Code

In any stretch of speech, linguistic and social information invariably occur together: whenever speech is produced, the listener can infer information about certain socio-indexical features of the speaker or the context (Foulkes & Docherty, 2006; see Section 5.1). With the growing awareness that socio-indexical features are always present in any stretch of speech has come the realization that the acquisition of these features by L2 learners is part and parcel of the L2 process. To comfortably handle a wide range of communicative contexts and social interactions in the L2, L2 learners need to be able to infer socio-indexical information about, for instance, regional or social background of the speaker. This observation presents us with the theoretical challenge of integrating the acquisition of socio-indexical information in models of L2 phonological acquisition. Chappell and Kanwit (2022), discussing L2 socio-phonetic variation, review the basic tenets of SLM, PAM-L2 and L2LP (cf. Section 2.2) and note that in none of those models is learner perception linked to social characteristics of the speakers (188). In other words, the models allow us to make testable predictions about how L2 learners will perceive L2 sounds on the basis of the relation to their L1 categories and how these learners may be able to acquire L2 categories through, for instance, boundary shifting, but they do not explain how learners come to link linguistic features in the L2 with social characteristics. If the L2 is viewed not just as a linguistic but also as a social code that learners need to master, then integrating social features into L2 speech learning models is vital. In this respect, it is worthwhile mentioning the Attrition & Drift in Access, Perception, and Production Theory (ADAPPT) recently proposed by De Leeuw and Chang (2024). This theory primarily focuses on the impact of additional languages on L1 speech, be it short-term, phonetic changes ('drift') or long-term, phonological ones ('attrition'). In general, ADAPPT stipulates that there will always be impact of additional language exposure (L2, L3, Lx) and acquisition on the L1, though the extent of the impact and the dimensions involved (access, perception or production) may vary. One of the principles of ADAPPT, outlined by De Leeuw and Chang (2024), specifically points at the way in which the social meaning of particular variables in the L1 will play a role in the extent to which they will be open or resistant to influence from an L2. The authors advocate that future studies on L1 drift and attrition should look into the social and indexical meanings in speakers' L1 and L2 in order to help explain which variables are affected. We believe that, similarly, the acquisition of L2 variables or features can be explained by their socio-indexical meaning and that theories or models focusing specifically on L2 acquisition should hence integrate sociolinguistic information.

The question then arises whether models on the acquisition of socio-lexical information can be integrated in existing L2 speech learning models, or whether new models need to be developed to cope with the development of L2 linguistic and social knowledge together. Chappel and Kanwit (2022), in their study on the L2 perception of aspiration (/s/ being realized as debuccalized [h]) in certain Spanish accents argue for a union of the L2 perception model they are using (L2LP) with exemplar models of phonological representation and indexical meaning (see Section 2.2 for a discussion on exemplar-based models). They argue that this unified model would account for how L2 learners first modify their L1 boundaries to the perception of the phonetic variants in the L2, after which these new categories can become exemplars in the learners' mental lexicon. What is needed for this last step to take place is sufficient exposure to the feature:

> Of course, a certain quantity of input is necessary to accomplish this feat, as learners cannot create exemplars until their L1 boundaries have shifted toward those of the L2. After learners gain experience in the L2, an indexical field can form as they connect individuals who produce coda [h] to socio-demographic categories, mapping this social information onto the exemplar stored in memory. (Chappell & Kanwit, 2022: 203)

In this view, the formation of exemplars thus hinges on the perception of the L2 categories. This would imply that less proficient L2 learners, who have not yet developed robust phonological representations in the L2, would be unable to acquire socio-indexical knowledge. This is in line with earlier studies in which it was shown that the development of sociophonetic knowledge goes hand in hand with an increase in proficiency level in the L2, as discussed in Section 5.2.3.

However, more research is needed to examine how powerful (in the sense of being able to formulate verifiable predictions) such a unified model would be.

Moreover, alternative models in which socio-indexical features are part of and are acquired hand in hand with phonological representations may need to be explored. Developing and testing predictions of L2 models that unify the acquisition of phonological representations and socio-indexical information presents a challenge for the future.

9 Conclusions and Implications

In closing, we draw attention to a number of implications of L2 phonology research that go beyond further insight into the theoretical question of how representations develop in L2 learners. We address the question of why the study of L2 phonological representations is relevant apart from its contribution to our understanding of issues in fundamental research.

A first implication relates to the domain of L2 instruction. In the following quote, Shea (2021) explicitly links L2 phonology to L2 pronunciation instruction:

> The field of L2 phonology studies the abstract representations created by L2 learners over the course of acquisition. L2 pronunciation, on the other hand, addresses concrete aspects of L2 speech, related primarily to intelligibility, comprehensibility, and accentedness (Munro and Derwing, 1995[a]). L2 phonology can be conceptualized as the frame in which L2 pronunciation develops or, where theory, data, and methods meet. In other words, pronunciation does not happen without phonology. (1)

In other words, if we want to develop L2 pronunciation instruction methods targeting intelligibility and comprehensibility, we need to understand how phonological representations develop in an L2, and what the role of variation is. Second language phonetic training studies in the framework of HPVT have shown that exposing learners to multiple, similar-sounding talkers facilitates the formation of L2 categories (see Section 3.2). Similarly, we can argue that exposure to different accents will enable L2 learners to build robust and flexible phonological representations, whose boundaries can move or loosen up when exposed to unfamiliar accents. In addition, learners will, after sufficient exposure to multiple speakers, be able to build knowledge of socio-indexical features in the L2, required to freely and successfully navigate in L2 communication contexts.

Secondly, studying the formation of phonological representations in the face of phonetic variation compels us to investigate in detail the specific features of accents, including regional and social, as well as L1 and L2 accents. Research on how L1 and L2 listeners perceive socio-indexical features and how these features may or may not impact intelligibility and – more generally – communication may also provide us with more insight into the causes of accent bias, defined by Watt, Levon and Ilbury (2023: 31) as 'a preference for one accent over others'. In Section 5.2.1 we reviewed earlier studies on accent recognition and bias in infants and children learning their L1, which provided evidence for the early occurrence of accent bias in children (Johnson et al., 2022). We mentioned how this bias could be due to social, but also to cognitive or linguistic factors. As is well known, accent bias persists into adulthood and Watt et al. even presume that it is universal, occurring in all speech communities large enough to have variation in accents. Once people's behaviour is influenced by their accent bias, in the sense that they will judge and treat speakers of a particular accent differently because of stereotypical ideas they have formed, the terms 'accent prejudice', 'accent discrimination' or simply 'accentism' are used (Watt et al., 2023: 31; see also The Accentism Project, a website with stories and materials about accent discrimination in the UK). The belief that some accents are 'better' or 'more accurate' than others – and that this is normal – is deeply rooted in society. One of the arguments often used to defend this view is that some (standard) accents are intrinsically clearer and more intelligible than others, related to listeners' higher familiarity with these accents (Watt et al., 2023). However, this belief, while widespread and popular, is not supported by scientific evidence. In fact, the general sociolinguistic viewpoint is that beliefs about different variants are based on social rather than linguistic judgements. In other words, it is the social status of the speakers of certain accents that will determine which accents are discriminated against and which ones are prestigious, either overtly or covertly (Lippi-Green, 2012). As a result, as pointed out by Ježek (2021), one and the same variant may be considered prestigious in one accent, but inferior in another. A case in point is that of (non-)rhoticity in accents of English: r-less pronunciations in words like 'car' carry high and low social prestige in different communities, and attitudes towards rhoticity have moreover changed over time (Becker, 2014). This illustrates that there is no clear link between linguistic variables and social attitudes. Studies that investigate the interplay between phonological representations, intelligibility and familiarity in L1 and L2 speakers and listeners and attitudes towards accent variation may therefore contribute to our understanding of the causes of accent bias and accent discrimination.

Finally, understanding the nature of phonological representations in L2 learning may be relevant for clinical linguistics studies on the development of phonological representations. Comparing results of studies involving typically developing L2 learners and atypically developing language learners may reveal similarities and differences that may help us to gain further insight into the nature of phonological representations in both populations. It is clear that any comparisons need to be made with caution, since processes in L2 learners may be different from those involved in speech acquisition by language users with an atypical development.

To conclude, in this Element we have delved into the field of L2 phonology with the aim of outlining the process through which L2 learners build L2 phonological representations in the face of phonetic variation inherent in speech. We have shown that building robust phonological representations is not a trivial task, especially because these representations also need to be flexible enough to deal with variation in the form of, for instance, regionally accented speech or social accents. We have provided evidence from empirical studies showing how accent variation impacts L2 phonological acquisition and have explored what clinical studies on individuals with atypical language development can tell us about the nature of phonological representations. We have furthermore argued that research in the field of sociophonetics, with empirical contributions to our understanding of how language learners acquire socio-indexical features, poses a challenge to current models of L2 phonology and speech learning, which need to be able to predict and test how language learners acquire both the linguistic and the socio-indexical features of the L2. We believe that future research that aims to include insights from sociophonetics and L2 acquisition will further our understanding of L2 phonological representations. Methods involving more spontaneous speech, in addition to lab speech, and larger data sets including speakers and listeners with a wide range of L1 and L2 backgrounds and regional and social accents will offer new insights and lead to a more holistic approach towards L2 phonology that does justice to the variable nature of speech.

References

Aksu, B. (2022). The influence of L1 Turkish regional dialects on L2 English speech production. Unpublished PhD dissertation, Lancaster University. https://eprints.lancs.ac.uk/id/eprint/182235/2/Amendment2022BaharPhD.pdf.

Alcorn, S., Meemann, K., Clopper, C. G. & Smiljanic, R. (2020). Acoustic cues and linguistic experience as factors in regional dialect classification. *Journal of the Acoustical Society of America*, 147, 657–670. https://doi.org/10.1121/1.4989083.

Alves, U. K. & Alcantara de Albuquerque, J. I. (2022). *Second Language Pronunciation: Different Approaches to Teaching and Training*. Berlin: De Gruyter Mouton. https://doi.org/10.1515/9783110736120.

Aoyama, K., Flege, J. E., Guion, S. G., Akahane-Yamada, R. & Yamada, T. (2004). Perceived phonetic dissimilarity and L2 speech learning: The case of Japanese /r/ and English /l/ and /r/. *Journal of Phonetics*, 32(2), 233–250. https://doi.org/10.1016/S0095-4470(03)00036-6.

Archibald, J. (2023). Phonological redeployment and the mapping problem: Cross-linguistic E-similarity is the beginning of the story, not the end. *Second Language Research*, 39(1), 287–297. https://doi.org/10.1177/02676583211066413.

Babel, M. (2012). Evidence for phonetic and social selectivity in spontaneous phonetic imitation. *Journal of Phonetics*, 40(1), 177–189. https://doi.org/10.1016/j.wocn.2011.09.001.

Baese-Berk, M. M., Chandrasekaran, B. & Roark, C. L. (2022). The nature of non-native speech sound representations. *Journal of the Acoustical Society of America*, 152(5), 3025–3034.

Baese-Berk, M. M., Kapnoula, E. C. & Samuel, A. G. (2024). The relationship of speech perception and speech production: It's complicated. *Psychonomic Bulletin & Review*. https://doi.org/10.3758/s13423-024-02561-w.

Baese-Berk, M. M., Levi, S. V. & Van Engen, K. J. (2023). Intelligibility as a measure of speech perception: Current approaches, challenges and recommendations. *Journal of the Acoustical Society of America*, 153(1), 68–76. https://doi.org/10.1121/10.0016806.

Barrientos, F. (2021). On segmental representations in second language phonology: A perceptual account. *Second Language Research*, 39(1), 259–285. https://doi.org/10.1177/02676583211030637.

Becker, K. (2014). (r) we there yet? The change of rhoticity in New York City English. *Language Variation and Change*, 26(2), 141–168. https://doi.org/10.1017/S0954394514000064.

Bent, T. & Baese-Berk, M. M. (2021). Perceptual learning of accented speech. In J. S. Pardo, L. C. Nygaard, R. E. Remez & D. B. Pisoni, eds., *The Handbook of Speech Perception*, 2nd edition. Hoboken, NJ: Wiley, pp. 428–464. https://doi.org/10.1002/9781119184096.CH16.

Bent, T. & Bradlow, A. R. (2003). The interlanguage speech intelligibility benefit. *Journal of the Acoustical Society of America*, 114(3), 1600–1610. https://doi.org/10.1121/1.1603234.

Best, C. (1995). A direct realist view of crosslanguage speech perception. In E. Strange, ed., *Speech Perception and Linguistic Experience: Theoretical and Methodological Issues*. Timonium, MD: New York Press, pp. 171–204.

Best, C. & Tyler, M. D. (2007). Nonnative and second-language speech perception: Commonalities and complementarities. In M. J. Munro & O.-S. Bohn, eds., *Second Language Speech Learning: The Role of Language Experience in Speech Perception and Production*. Amsterdam: John Benjamins, pp. 13–34.

Bishop, D. V. M. & Snowling, M. J. (2004). Developmental dyslexia and specific language impairment: Same or different? *Psychological Bulletin*, 130(6), 858–886. https://doi.org/10.1037/0033-2909.130.6.858.

Bordag D., Gor, K. & Opitz, A. (2022). Ontogenesis model of the L2 lexical representation. *Bilingualism: Language and Cognition*, 25, 185–201. https://doi.org/10.1017/S1366728921000250.

Breitbarth, A., Ghyselen, A.-S., van Hout, R. & Wieling, M. (2023). Big data: New perspectives for research on language variation and change. *Taal en Tongval*, 75(1), 1–6. https://doi.org/10.5117/TET2023.1.001.BREI.

Broersma, M. (2005). Perception of familiar contrasts in unfamiliar positions. *Journal of the Acoustical Society of America*, 117(6), 3890–3901. https://doi.org/10.1121/1.1906060.

Browman. C. & Goldstein, I. (1986). Towards an articulatory phonology. *Phonology Yearbook*, 3, 219–252.

Browman, C. & Goldstein, L. (1992). Articulatory phonology: An overview. *Phonetica*, 49(3–4), 155–180. https://doi.org/10.1159/000261913.

Bruggeman L. & Cutler, A. (2019). No L1 privilege in talker adaptation. *Bilingualism: Language and Cognition*, 23(3), 681–693. https://doi.org/10.1017/S1366728919000646.

Catanzariti, B. & Currie, M. eds. (2022). How to use Mechanical Turk ethically [how-to guide]. Sage Research Methods: Doing Research Online. https://doi.org/10.4135/9781529608403.

Chang, C. B. (2012). Rapid and multifaceted effects of second-language learning on first-language speech production. *Journal of Phonetics*, 40(2), 249–268.

Chang, C. B. (2013). A novelty effect in phonetic drift of the native language. *Journal of Phonetics*, 41(6), 520–533.

Chang, C. B. (2019). Phonetic drift. In M. S. Schmid & B. Köpke, eds., *The Oxford Handbook of Language Attrition*. Oxford: Oxford University Press, pp. 191–203.

Chappell, W. & Kanwit, M. (2022). Do learners connect sociophonetic variation with regional and social characteristics? The case of L2 perception of Spanish aspiration. *Studies in Second Language Acquisition*, 44(1), 185–209. https://doi.org/10.1017/S0272263121000115.

Cherry, E. C. (1953). Some experiments on the recognition of speech, with one and with two ears. *Journal of the Acoustical Society of America*, 25(5), 975–979.

Chládková, K., Boersma, P. & Escudero, P. (2022). Unattended distributional training can shift phoneme boundaries. *Bilingualism: Language and Cognition*, 25(5), 827–840. https://doi.org/10.1017/S1366728922000086.

Chládková, K. & Podlipský, V. J. (2011). Native dialect matters: Perceptual assimilation of Dutch vowels by Czech listeners. *Journal of the Acoustical Society of America*, 130(4), 186–192. https://doi.org/10.1121/1.3629135.

Claessen, M., & Leitão, S. (2012). Phonological representations in children with SLI. *Child Language Teaching and Therapy*, 28(2), 211–223. https://doi.org/10.1177/0265659012436851.

Clopper, C. G. (2004). Linguistic experience and the perceptual classification of dialect variation. Unpublished PhD thesis, University of Indiana.

Clopper, C. G. (2021). Perception of dialect variation. In J. S. Pardo, L. C. Nygaard, R. E. Remez & D. B. Pisoni, eds., *The Handbook of Speech Perception*, 2nd edition. Hoboken, NJ: Wiley. https://doi.org/10.1002/9781119184096.ch13.

Clopper, C. G. & Bradlow, A. R. (2009). Free classification of American English dialects by native and nonnative listeners. *Journal of Phonetics*, 37(4), 436–451. https://doi.org/10.1016/j.wocn.2009.07.004.

Clopper, C. G. & Dossey, E. (2020). Phonetic convergence to Southern American English: Acoustics and perception. *Journal of the Acoustical Society of America*, 147(1), 671–683. https://doi.org/10.1121/10.0000555.

Cohn, A. C., Fougeron, C. & Huffman, M. K. (2017). Laboratory phonology. In *The Routledge Handbook of Phonological Theory*, 1st edition. Abingdon: Routledge, pp. 504–529. https://doi.org/10.4324/9781315675428-18.

Cohn, A. C. & Renwick, M. (2019). Doing phonology in the age of big data. *Cornell Working Papers in Linguistics.* https://doi.org/10.5281/zenodo.3725897.

Coquillon, A. (2007). Le français parlé à Marseille: Exemple d'un locuteur PFC. *Bulletin PFC (Phonologie du Français Contemporain)*, 7, 145–156.

Coquillon, A. (2010). Conversation à Marseille (Bouches-du-Rhône): Un cuisinier dans la marine. In S. Detey, J. Durand, B. Laks & C. Lyche, eds., *Les variétés du français parlé dans l'espace francophone: Ressources pour l'enseignement.* Paris: Ophrys, pp. 117–129.

Cox, F. & Palethorpe, S. (2007). Australian English. *Journal of the International Phonetic Association*, 37(3), 341–350.

Cutler, A. & Otake, T. (2004). Pseudo-homophony in non-native listening. *Journal of the Acoustical Society of America*, 115, 2392. https://doi.org/10.1121/1.4780547.

Dahan, D., Drucker, S. J. & Scarborough, R. A. (2008). Talker adaptation in speech perception: Adjusting the signal or the representations? *Cognition*, 108, 710–718. https://doi.org/10.1016/j.cognition.2008.06.003.

Dailey, M. (2024). Late Bilingual Perception of Phonetic and Sociophonetic Cues. Doctoral dissertation. Ecole normale supérieure – Paris Sciences et Lettres.

Darcy. I. (2022). From fuzzy to fine-grained representations in the developing lexicon. *Bilingualism: Language and Cognition*, 25, 206–207. https://doi.org/10.1017/S1366728921000572.

De Haes, H., Peperkamp, S., Crible, L. & Simon, E. (in prep.). Real-time reactions to sociophonetic features in French accents.

De Leeuw, E. & Chang, C. B. (2024). Phonetic and phonological L1 attrition and drift in bilingual speech. In M. Amengual, ed., *The Cambridge Handbook of Bilingual Phonetics and Phonology.* Cambridge: Cambridge University Press, pp. 721–745.

Delvaux, V. & Soquet, A. (2007). The influence of ambient speech on adult speech productions through unintentional imitation. *Phonetica*, 64(2–3), 145–173. https://doi.org/10.1159/000107914.

Diehl, R. L. (1992). *Articulatory Phonology*, Special Topic Issue, 49(3–4).

Eimas, P. D. & Corbit, J. D. (1973). Selective adaptation of linguistic feature detectors. *Cognitive Psychology*, 4(1), 99–109. https://doi.org/10.1016/0010-0285(73)90006-6.

Eisenstein, M. (1982). A study of social variation in adult second language acquisition. *Language Learning*, 32, 367–391.

Ellis, N. C. (2022). Fuzzy representations. *Bilingualism: Language and Cognition*, 25(2), 210–211. https://doi.org/10.1017/S1366728921000638.

Elman, J. L., Diehl, R. L. & Buchwald, S. E. (1977). Perceptual switching in bilinguals. *Journal of the Acoustical Society of America*, 62, 971.

Elvin, J., Escudero, P. & Vasiliev, P. (2014). Spanish is better than English for discriminating Portuguese vowels: Acoustic similarity versus vowel inventory size. *Frontiers in Psychology*, 5, 103389.

Ernestus, M. & Baayen, R. H. (2007). The comprehension of acoustically reduced morphologically complex words: The roles of deletion, duration, and frequency of occurrence. In J. Trouvain & W. J. Barry, eds., *Proceedings of the 16th International Congress of Phonetic Sciences*. Saarbrucken: Saarland University, pp. 773–776.

Escudero, P. (2005). Linguistic perception and second language acquisition: Explaining the attainment of optimal phonological categorization. PhD thesis. LOT Dissertation Series 113. Utrecht University.

Escudero, P. & Boersma, P. (2004). Bridging the gap between L2 speech perception research and phonological theory. *Studies in Second Language Acquisition*, 26(4), 551–585. https://doi.org/10.1017/S0272263104040021.

Escudero P. & Hayes-Harb, R. (2022). The Ontogenesis Model may provide a useful guiding framework, but lacks explanatory power for the nature and development of L2 lexical representation. *Bilingualism: Language and Cognition*, 25, 212–213. https://doi.org/10.1017/S1366728921000602.

Escudero, P., Simon, E. & Mitterer, H. (2012). The perception of English front vowels by North Holland and Flemish listeners: Acoustic similarity predicts and explains cross-linguistic and L2 perception. *Journal of Phonetics*, 40(2), 280–288. https://doi.org/10.1016/j.wocn.2011.11.004.

Escudero, P. & Williams, D. (2012). Native dialect influences second-language vowel perception: Peruvian versus Iberian Spanish learners of Dutch. *Journal of the Acoustical Society of America*, 131, EL406–EL412.

Evans, B. G. & Iverson, P. (2007). Plasticity in vowel perception and production: A study of accent change in young adults. *Journal of the Acoustical Society of America*, 121(6), 3814–3826. https://doi.org/10.1121/1.2722209.

Fanelli, D. (2012). Negative results are disappearing from most disciplines and countries. *Scientometrics*, 90(3), 891–904.

Fishero, S., Jongman, A. & Sereno, J. A. (2023). Perception and production of Mandarin-accented English: The effect of degree of accentedness on the Interlanguage Speech Intelligibility Benefit for Listeners (ISIB-L) and Talkers (ISIB-T). *Journal of Phonetics*, 99, 1–18.

Flege, J. E. (1995). Second language speech learning: Theory, findings, and problems. In W. Strange, ed., *Speech Perception and Linguistic Experience: Issues in Cross-Language Research*. Timonium, MD: York Press, pp. 233–277. http://doi.org/10.1111/j.1600-0404.1995.tb01710.x.

Flege, J. (2021). New methods for second language (L2) speech research. In R. Wayland, ed., *Second Language Speech Learning: Theoretical and Empirical Progress*. Cambridge: Cambridge University Press, pp. 119–156. https://doi.org/10.1017/9781108886901.004.

Flege, J. E. & Bohn, O.-S. (2021). *Second Language Speech learning: Theoretical and Empirical Progress*, ed. R. Wayland. Cambridge: Cambridge University Press, pp. 3–83.

Flege, J. E. & Eefting, W. (1987). Cross-language switching in stop consonant perception and production by Dutch speakers of English. *Speech Communication*, 6(3), 185–202.

Flege, J. E., Munro, M. J. & MacKay, I. (1995). Effects of second-language learning on the production of English consonants, *Speech Communication*, 16, 1–26.

Foulkes, P. & Docherty, G. (2006). The social life of phonetics and phonology. *Journal of Phonetics*, 34(4), 409–438. https://doi.org/10.1016/j.wocn.2005.08.002.

Foulkes, H. & Hay, J. B. (2015). The emergence of sociophonetic structure. In B. MacWhinney & W. O'Grady, eds., *The Handbook of Language Emergence*. Wiley, pp. 292–313. https://doi.org/10.1002/9781118346136.ch13.

Fox, R. A. & McGory, J. T. (2007). Second language acquisition of a regional dialect of American English by native Japanese speakers. In O.-S. Bohn & M. J. Munro, eds., *Language Experience in Second Language Speech Learning*. Amsterdam: John Benjamins, pp. 117–134.

Frisch, S. A. (2017). Exemplar theories in phonology. In S. J. Hannahs and A. R. K. Bosch, eds., *The Routledge Handbook of Phonological Theory*. Abingdon: Routledge, pp. 553–568.

Ganong, W. F. (1980). Phonetic categorization in auditory word perception. *Journal of Experimental Psychology: Human Perception and Performance*, 6(1), 110–125. https://doi.org/10.1037/0096-1523.6.1.110.

Gnevsheva, K. (2022). Studying sociophonetics in second languages. In K. Geeslin, ed., *The Routledge Handbook of Second Language Acquisition and Sociolinguistics*. Routledge, pp. 189–199. https://doi.org/10.4324/9781003017325-18.

Gnevsheva, K., Szakay, A. & Jansen, S. (2021). Phonetic convergence across dialect boundaries in first and second language speakers. *Journal of Phonetics*, 89, 101110. https://doi.org/10.1016/j.wocn.2021.101110.

Goldrick, M. & Cole, J. (2023). Advancement of phonetics in the 21st century: Exemplar models of speech production. *Journal of Phonetics*, 99, 101254. https://doi.org/10.1016/j.wocn.2023.101254.

Guediche, S., Blumstein, S. E., Fiez, J. A. & Holt, L. L. (2014). Speech perception under adverse conditions: Insights from behavioral, computational, and neuroscience research. *Frontiers in Systems Neuroscience*, 7(126), 1–16. https://doi.org/10.3389/fnsys.2013.00126.

Guion, S. G. (2003). The vowel systems of Quichua–Spanish bilinguals. *Phonetica*, 60(2), 98–128. https://doi.org/10.1159/000071449.

Gunter, K. M., Vaughn, C. R., Tyler, M. & Kendall, S. (2022). Contextualising /s/ retraction: Sibilant variation and change in Washington D.C. African American language. *Language Variation and Change*, 33(3), 331–357. https://doi.org/10.1017/S095439452100020X.

Hayes-Harb, R., Smith, B. L., Bent, T. & Bradlow, A. R. (2008). The interlanguage speech intelligibility benefit for native speakers of Mandarin: Production and perception of English word-final voicing contrasts. *Journal of Phonetics*, 36(4), 664–679. https://doi.org/10.1016/j.wocn.2008.04.002.

Janson, T. (1983). Sound change in perception and production. *Language*, 59, 18–34.

Ježek, M. (2021). *Sociophonology of Received Pronunciation: Native and Non-native Environments*. Brno: Masaryk University Press. https://digilib.phil.muni.cz/sites/default/files/pdf/143839-monography.pdf. https://doi.org/10.5817/CZ.MUNI.M210-9833-2021.

Jiang, F. & Kennison, S. (2022). The impact of L2 English learners' belief about an interlocutor's English proficiency on L2 phonetic accommodation. *Journal of Psycholinguistic Research*, 51, 217–234. https://doi.org/10.1007/s10936-021-09835-7.

Johnson, E., van Heugten, M. & Buckler, H. (2022). Navigating accent variation: A developmental perspective. *Annual Review of Linguistics*, 8, 365–387. https://doi.org/10.1146/annurev-linguistics-032521-053717.

Johnson, K. (1997). Speech perception without speaker normalization: An exemplar model. In K. Johnson & J. W. Mullennix, eds., *Talker Variability in Speech Processing*. San Diego, CA: Academic Press, pp. 145–166.

Johnson, K. (2007). Decisions and mechanisms in exemplar-based phonology. In M. J. Solé, P. Beddor & M. Ohala, eds., *Experimental Approaches to Phonology: In Honor of John Ohala*. Oxford: Oxford University Press, pp. 25–40.

Johnson, K. (2020). The ΔF method of vocal tract length normalization for vowels. *Laboratory Phonology*, 11(1), 1–16. https://doi.org/10.5334/labphon.196.

Kachru, B. B. (1985). Standards, codification and sociolinguistic realism: The English language in the outer circle. In R. Quirk & H. G. Widdowson, eds.,

English in the World: Teaching and Learning the Language and Literatures. Cambridge: Cambridge University Press, pp. 11–30.

Kartushina, N. & Frauenfelder, U. H. (2013). On the role of L1 speech production in L2 perception: Evidence from Spanish learners of French. Paper presented at Interspeech 2013, Lyon, France.

Kattner, F. & Ellermeier, W. (2020). Distraction at the cocktail party: Attenuation of the irrelevant speech effect after a training of auditory selective attention. *Journal of Experimental Psychology: Human Perception and Performance*, 46(1), 10–20. https://doi.org/10.1037/xhp0000695.

Kendall, T. & Fridland, V. (2021). *Sociophonetics* (Key Topics in Sociolinguistics). Cambridge: Cambridge University Press. https://doi.org/10.1017/9781316809709.

Kendall, T., Pharao, N., Stuart-Smith, J. & Vaughn, C. (2023). Advancements of phonetics in the 21st century: Theoretical issues in sociophonetics. *Journal of Phonetics*, 98. https://doi.org/10.1016/j.wocn.2023.101226.

Kennedy, S. & Trofimovich, P. (2008). Intelligibility, comprehensibility, and accentedness of L2 speech: The role of listener experience and semantic context. *Canadian Modern Language Review*, 64(3), 459–489.

Kihlstrom, J. F. (2021). Ecological validity and 'ecological validity'. *Perspectives on Psychological Science*, 16(2), 466–471. https://doi.org/10.1177/1745691620966791.

Kriengwatana, B., Terry, J., Chladkova, K. & Escudero, P. (2016). Speaker and accent variation are handled differently: Evidence in native and non-native listeners. *PLoS ONE*, 11(6), e0156870. https://doi.org/10.1371/journal.pone.0156870.

Kuhl, P. K. (1992). Infants' perception and representation of speech: Development of a new theory. *Proceedings of the Second International Conference on Spoken Language Processing* (ICSLP), 449–456. https://doi.org/10.21437/ICSLP.1992-3.

Kwon, H., MacLeod, B. & Nielsen, K. (2024). Phonetic imitation: Representation, sound change, and other theoretical implications. Satellite workshop at the 19th Conference on Laboratory Phonology: LabPhon 19, Hanyang University, Seoul, 27–29 June. https://labphon.org/labphon19/phonetic-imitation.

Laase, M. (2015). Vowel production in children and adults with Williams syndrome. Unpublished honours thesis. Ohio State University.

Lavan, N. (2023). Person perception from voices: Impressions of physical, trait, and social characteristics emerge with 800 ms of exposure. *Psychological Science*, 34(7), 771–783. https://doi.org/10.31234/osf.io/7rzem.

Lee, D. & Baese-Berk, M. M. (2021). Non-native English listeners' adaptation to native English speakers. *Journal of the Acoustical Society of America: Express Letters*, 1(10), 105201. https://doi.org/10.1121/10.0006558.

Lemhöfer K. (2022). What is fuzziness, and how much does it explain? *Bilingualism: Language and Cognition*, 25, 222–223. https://doi.org/10.1017/S1366728921000596.

Lenneberg, E. H. (1967). *Biological Foundations of Language*. New York: Wiley.

Levi, S. V. (2021). Perception of indexical properties of speech by children. In J. S. Pardo, L. C. Nygaard, R. E. Remez & D. B. Pisoni, eds., *The Handbook of Speech Perception*, 2nd edition. Wiley, pp. 465–483. https://doi.org/10.1002/9781119184096.ch17.

Li, M. Y. C., Braze, D., Kukona, A., Johns, C. L., Tabor, W., van Dyke, J. A., Mencl, W. E., Shankweiler, D. P., Pugh, K. R. & Magnuson, J. S. (2019). Individual differences in subphonemic sensitivity and phonological skills. *Journal of Memory & Language*, 107, 195–215. https://doi.org/10.1016/j.jml.2019.03.008.

Liberman, A. M., Cooper, F. S., Shankweiler, D. P. & Studdert-Kennedy, M. (1967). Perception of the speech code. *Psychological Review*, 74(6), 431–461. https://doi.org/10.1037/h0020279.

Liberman, A. M. & Mattingly, I. G. (1985). The motor theory of speech perception revised. *Cognition*, 21(1), 1–36.

Lippi-Green, R. (1994). Accent, standard language ideology, and discriminatory pretext in the courts. *Language in Society*, 23(2), 163–198. https://doi.org/10.1017/S0047404500017826.

Lippi-Green, R. (2011). *English with an Accent: Language, Ideology and Discrimination in the United States*, 2nd edition. London: Routledge. https://doi.org/10.4324/9780203348802.

Long, G. B., Fox, R. A. & Jacewicz, E. (2016). Dyslexia limits the ability to categorize talker dialect. *Journal of Speech, Language and Hearing Research*, 59, 900–914. https://doi.org/10.1044/2016_JSLHR-S-15-0106.

Lu, J. & Ota, M. (2023). The effect of learning context on Mandarin listeners' perception of English vowels. *Proceedings of the 20th International Congress of the Phonetic Sciences*, 2572–2575.

MacLeod, B. & Di Lonardo Burr, S. M. (2022). Phonetic imitation of the acoustic realization of stress in Spanish: Production and perception. *Journal of Phonetics*, 92, 101139. https://doi.org/10.1016/j.wocn.2022.101139.

Maillart, C., Schelstraete, M.-A. & Hupet, M. (2004). Phonological representations of children with SLI: A study of French. *Journal of Speech, Hearing and Language Research*, 47, 187–198. https://doi.org/10.1044/1092-4388(2004/016).

Mattys, S., Davis, M. H., Bradlow, A. R. & Scott, S. K. (2012). Speech recognition in adverse conditions: A review. *Language and Cognitive Processes*, 27 (7–8), 953–978. https://doi.org/10.1080/01690965.2012.705006.

Maye J., Werker J. F. & Gerken, L. (2002). Infant sensitivity to distributional information can affect phonetic discrimination. *Cognition*, 82(3), B101–B111. https://doi.org/10.1016/s0010-0277(01)00157-3.

Melguy, Y. V. & Johnson, K. (2021). General adaptation to accented English: Speech intelligibility unaffected by perceived source of non-native accent. *Journal of the Acoustical Society of America*, 149(4), 2602–2614. https://doi.org/10.1121/10.0004240.

Melguy, Y. V. & Johnson, K. (2022). Perceptual adaptation to a novel accent: Phonetic category expansion or category shift? *Journal of the Acoustical Society of America*, 152, 2090. https://doi.org/10.1121/10.0014602.

Mennen, I., Reubold, U., Endes, K. & Mayr, R. (2022). Plasticity of native intonation in the L1 of English migrants to Austria. *Languages*, 7(3), 1–27. https://doi.org/10.3390/languages7030241.

Mitterer, H. & McQueen, J. (2009). Foreign subtitles help but native-language subtitles harm foreign speech perception. *PloS ONE*, 4. e7785. https://doi.org/10.1371/journal.pone.0007785.

Mitterer, H. & Müsseler, J. (2013). Regional accent variation in the shadowing task: Evidence for a loose perception–action coupling in speech. *Attention, Perception, & Psychophysics*, 75(3), 557–575. https://doi.org/10.3758/s13414-012-0407-8.

Mitterer, H., Reinisch, E. & McQueen, J. M. (2018). Allophones, not phonemes in spoken-word recognition. *Journal of Memory and Language*, 98, 77–92. https://doi.org/10.1016/j.jml.2017.09.005.

Montgomery, C. & Moore, E. F. (2018). Evaluating s(c)illy voices: The effects of salience, stereotypes, and co-present language variables on real-time reactions to regional speech. *Language*, 94(3), 629–661.

Mora, J. C. (2007). Methodological issues in assessing L2 perceptual phonological competence. In *Proceedings of the PTLC 2007 Phonetics Teaching and Learning Conference*. London: Department of Phonetics and Linguistics, University College London, pp. 1–5.

Moyer, A. (1999). Ultimate attainment in L2 phonology. The critical factors of age, motivation, and instruction. *Studies in Second Language Acquisition*, 21, 81–108. https://doi.org/10.1017/S0272263199001035.

Munro, M. J. (2008). Foreign accent and speech intelligibility. In J. G. H. Edwards & M. L. Zampini (eds.), *Phonology and Second Language Acquisition*. Amsterdam: John Benjamins, pp. 193–218.

Munro, M. J. & Derwing, T. M. (1995a). Foreign accent, comprehensibility, and intelligibility in the speech of second language learners. *Language Learning*, 45, 73–97. https://doi.org/10.1111/j.1467-1770.1995.tb00963.

Munro, M. J. & Derwing, T. M. (1995b). Processing time, accent, and comprehensibility in the perception of native and foreign-accented speech. *Language and Speech*, 38, 289–306. https://doi.org/10.1177/002383099503800305.

Munro, M. J. & Derwing, T. M. (2020). Foreign accent, comprehensibility and intelligibility, redux. *Journal of Second Language Pronunciation*, 6(3), 283–309. https://doi.org/10.1075/jslp.20038.mun.

Nagle, C. L. & Baese-Berk, M. M. (2022). Advancing the state of the art in L2 speech perception-production research: Revisiting theoretical assumptions and methodological practices. *Studies in Second Language Acquisition*, 44(2), 580–605. https://doi.org/10.1017/S0272263121000371.

Nazzi, T., Jusczyk, P. W. & Johnson, E. K. (2000). Language discrimination by English-learning 5-month-olds: Effects of rhythm and familiarity. *Journal of Memory and Language*, 43, 1–19. https://doi.org/10.1006/jmla.2000.2698.

Nicol, J. (2022). How fuzzy are L2 phonological representations? *Bilingualism: Language and Cognition*, 25, 230–231. https://doi.org/10.1017/S1366728921000614.

Nielsen, K. (2011). Specificity and abstractness of VOT imitation. *Journal of Phonetics*, 39, 132–142. https://doi.org/10.1016/j.wocn.2010.12.007.

Norris, D., McQueen, J. M. & Cutler, A. (2003). Perceptual learning in speech. *Cognitive Psychology*, 47(2), 204–238. https://doi.org/10.1016/S0010-0285(03)00006-9.

Nycz, J. (2013). Changing words or changing rules? Second dialect acquisition and phonological representation. *Journal of Phonetics*, 52, 49–62. https://doi.org/10.1016/j.pragma.2012.12.014.

Nycz, J. (2015). Second dialect acquisition: A sociophonetic perspective. *Language and Linguistic Compass*, 9(11), 469–482. https://doi.org/10.1080/23268263.2020.1723359.

Owren, M. J., Berkowitz, M. & Bachorowski, J. A. (2007). Listeners judge talker sex more efficiently from male than from female vowels. *Perception & Psychophysics*, 69(6), 930–941. https://doi.org/10.3758/bf03193930.

Pan, N. & Chen, L. (2005). Phonological/phonemic awareness and reading: A crosslinguistic perspective. *Journal of Multilingual Communication Disorders*, 3, 145–152. http://dx.doi.org/10.1080/14769670500066271.

Pardo, J. S., Gibbons, R., Suppes, A. & Krauss, R. M. (2012). Phonetic convergence in college roommates. *Journal of Phonetics*, 40(1), 190–197. https://doi.org/10.1016/J.WOCN.2011.10.001.

Perrachione, T. K., Del Tufo, S. N. & Gabrieli, J. D. (2011). Human voice recognition depends on language ability. *Science*, 333, 595. https://doi.org/10.1126/science.1207327.

Phonology du Français Contemporain, corpus of spoken French available at FLORAL-PFC – Base de données sur le français oral contemporain dans l'espace francophone (projet-pfc.net).

Pierrehumbert, J. (2016). Phonological representation: Beyond abstract versus episodic. *Annual Review of Linguistics*, 2, 33–52. https://doi.org/10.1146/annurev-linguist-030514-125050.

Polka, L., & Werker, J. F. (1994). Developmental changes in perception of nonnative vowel contrasts. *Journal of Experimental Psychology: Human Perception and Performance*, 20, 421–435.

Rato, A. & Oliveira, D. (2022). Assessing the robustness of L2 perceptual training: A closer look at generalization and retention of learning. In U. Alves & J. Albuquerque, eds., *Second Language Pronunciation: Different Approaches to Teaching and Training*. Berlin: De Gruyter Mouton, pp. 369–396. https://doi.org/10.1515/9783110736120-014.

Rebernik, T., Jacobi, J., Jonkers, R., Noiray, A. & Wieling, M. (2021). A review of data collection practices using electromagnetic articulography. *Laboratory Phonology: Journal of the Association for Laboratory Phonology*, 12(1.6), 1–42. https://doi.org/10.5334/labphon.237.

Rodd, J. M. (2024). Moving experimental psychology online: How to obtain high quality data when we can't see our participants. *Journal of Memory and Language*, 134, 104472. https://doi.org/10.1016/j.jml.2023.104472.

Saito, K., Trofimovich, P. & Isaacs, T. (2017). Using listener judgements to investigate linguistic influences on L2 comprehensibility and accentedness: A validation and generalization study. *Applied Linguistics*, 38(4), 439–462. https://doi.org/10.1093/applin/amv047.

Sancier, M. L. & Fowler, C. A. (1997). Gestural drift in a bilingual speaker of Brazilian Portuguese and English. *Journal of Phonetics*, 25(4), 421–436.

Sarampalis, A., Kalluri, S., Edwards, B. & Hafter, E. (2009). Objective measures of listening effort: Effects of background noise and noise reduction. *Journal of Speech Language and Hearing Research*, 52, 1230–1240.

Schmidt, R. W. (1990). The role of consciousness in second language learning. *Applied Linguistics*, 11, 129–158.

Scobbie, J., Turk, A., Geng, C., King, S., Lickley, R. & Richmond, K. (2013). The Edinburgh Speech Production Facility DoubleTalk corpus. In *Proceedings Interspeech 2013*. www.isca-archive.org/interspeech_2013/scobbie13_interspeech.pdf.

Shea C. E. (2021). Commentary: L2 phonology: Where theory, data, and methods meet. *Frontiers in Psychology*, 12, 1–3. https://doi.org/10.3389/fpsyg.2021.774721.

Sheldon, A. & Strange, W. (1982). The acquisition of /r/ and /l/ by Japanese learners of English: Evidence that speech production can precede speech perception. *Applied Psycholinguistics*, 3, 243–261.

Simon, E. (2010). *Voicing in Contrast: Acquiring a Second Language Laryngeal System*. Ginkgo: Academia Press. https://doi.org/10.26530/OAPEN_377758.

Simon, E., Debaene, M. & Van Herreweghe, M. (2015). The effect of L1 regional variation on the perception and production of standard L1 and L2 vowels. *Folia Linguistica*, 49(2), 521–553. https://doi.org/10.1515/flin-2015-0018.

Simon, E., De Clercq, B. & Degrave, P. (in prep.). Listening to regional accents: Dutch and French listeners' perception of phonetic vowel variation in Belgian Dutch.

Simon, E., De Clercq, B., Degrave, P. & Decourcelle, Q. (2022). On the robustness of high variability phonetic training effects: A study on the perception of non-native Dutch contrasts by French-speaking learners. In U. K. Alves & J. Imaregna Alcantara de Albuquerque (eds.), *Second Language Pronunciation*, Vol. 64. Berlin: De Gruyter Mouton, pp. 315–344. https://doi.org/10.1515/9783110736120-012.

Simon, E., Lybaert, C. & Plevoets, K. (2022). Social attitudes, intelligibility and comprehensibility: The role of the listener in the perception of non-native speech. *Vial-Vigo International Journal of Applied Linguistics*, 19, 177–221. https://doi.org/10.35869/vial.v0i19.3763.

Simon, E., Sjerps, M. & Fikkert, P. (2014). Phonological representations in children's native and non-native lexicon. *Bilingualism: Language and Cognition*, 17(1), 3–21. https://doi.org/10.1017/S1366728912000764.

Solon, M. & Kanwit, M. (2022). New methods for tracking development of sociophonetic competence: Exploring a preference task for Spanish /d/ deletion. *Applied Linguistics*, 43(4), 805–825. https://doi.org/10.1093/applin/amac009.

Solon, M., Linford, B. & Geeslin, K. L. (2018). Acquisition of sociophonetic variation: Intervocalic /d/ reduction in native and non-native Spanish. *Revista Española de Lingüística Aplicada/Spanish Journal of Applied Linguistics*, 31, 309–344. https://doi.org/10.1075/resla.16028.sol.

Stephan, C. (1997). The unknown Englishes? Testing German students' ability to identify varieties of English. In E. W. Schneider, ed., *Englishes around the World*. Amsterdam: John Benjamins, pp. 93–108.

Stewart, N., Chandler, J. & Paolacci, G. (2017). Crowdsourcing samples in cognitive science. *Trends in Cognitive Sciences*, 21(10), 736–748. https://doi.org/10.1016/j.tics.2017.06.007.

Strycharczuk, P. & Scobbie, J. M. (2017). Fronting of Southern British English high-back vowels in articulation and acoustics. *Journal of the Acoustical Society of America*, 142 (1), 322. https://doi.org/10.1121/1.4991010.

Swan D. & Goswami, U. (1997). Phonological awareness deficits in developmental dyslexia and the phonological representations hypothesis. *Journal of Experimental Child Psychology*, 66(1), 18–41. https://doi.org/10.1006/jecp.1997.2375. PMID: 9226932.

Thomas, E. R. (2013). Sociophonetics. In J. K. Chambers & N. Schilling-Estes, eds., *The Handbook of Language Variation and Change*, 2nd edition. Oxford: Wiley-Blackwell, pp. 108–127.

Tilsen, S. (2016). Selection and coordination: The articulatory basis for the emergence of phonological structure. *Journal of Phonetics*, 55, 53–77. https://doi.org/10.1016/j.wocn.2015.11.005.

Tucker, B. V. & Mukai, Y. (2023). *Spontaneous Speech*. Cambridge Elements in Phonetics. Cambridge: Cambridge University Press. https://doi.org/10.1017/9781108943024.

Turner, J. (2022). Analysing the relationship between L2 production and different stages of L2 processing: Eye-tracking and acoustic evidence for a novel contrast. *Journal of Phonetics*, 91, 101–134. https://doi.org/10.1016/j.wocn.2022.101134.

Turner, J. (2024). The role of L2 input in developing a novel L2 contrast phonetically and phonologically: Production evidence from a residence abroad context. *Second Language Research*, 0(0). https://doi.org/10.1177/02676583231217166.

Tyler, M. (2019). PAM-L2 and phonological category acquisition in the foreign language classroom. In A. M. Nyvad, M. Hejná, A. Højen, A. B. Jespersen & M. H. Sørensen (eds.), *A Sound Approach to Language Matters: In Honor of Ocke-Schwen Bohn*. Aarhus: Aarhus University Press, pp. 607–630.

van de Velde, H., Pinget, A., Voeten, C. & Demolin, D. (2022). Laboratory sociolinguistics. In G. Kristiansen, K. Franco, S. de Pascale, L. Rosseel & W. Zhang, eds., *Cognitive Sociolinguistics Revisited*. Berlin: De Gruyter Mouton, pp. 557–571. https://doi.org/10.1515/9783110733945-045.

van de Velde, H. & van Hout, R. (2000). N-deletion in reading style. In H. de Hoop & T. van der Wouden, eds., *Linguistics in the Netherlands 2000*. Amsterdam: John Benjamins, pp. 209–219.

van Heugten, M. & Johnson, E. K. (2014). Learning to contend with accents in infancy: Benefits of brief speaker exposure. *Journal of Experimental Psychology: General*, 143(1), 340–350. https://doi.org/10.1037/a0032192.

van Heugten, M. & Johnson, E. K. (2016). Toddlers' word recognition in an unfamiliar regional accent: The role of local sentence context and prior accent exposure. *Language and Speech*, 59(3), 353–363. https://10.1177/0023830915600471.

van Heugten, M., Paquette-Smith, M., Krieger, D. R. & Johnson, E. K. (2018). Infants' recognition of foreign-accented words: Flexible yet precise signal-to-word mapping strategies. *Journal of Memory and Language*, 100, 51–60. https://doi.org/10.1016/j.jml.2018.01.003.

van Leussen, J.-W. & Escudero, P. (2015). Learning to perceive and recognize a second language: The L2LP model revised. *Frontiers in Psychology*, 6, 103694.

Verbeke, G. (2024). On the role of ecological validity in language and speech research. In J. Buysschaert & A. Lefèvre, eds., *Taalkunde nu*. Gent: Skribis. Series Studia Germanica Gandensia (Libri) & Spieghel Historiael, pp. 69–95.

Verbeke, G., Mitterer, H. & Simon, E. (2025). Phonetic reduction in native and non-native English speech: Assessing the intelligibility for L2 listeners. *Bilingualism, Language and Cognition*. https://doi.org/10.1017/S1366728925000021.

Verbeke, G. & Simon, E. (2023a). Listening to accents: Comprehensibility, accentedness and intelligibility of native and non-native English speech. *Lingua*, 292, 103572. https://doi.org/10.1016/j.lingua.2023.103572.

Verbeke, G. & Simon, E. (2023b). Replication data for Listening to Accents: Comprehensibility, accentedness and intelligibility of native and non-native English speech, DataverseNO, V1. https://doi.org/10.18710/8F0Q0L.

Vriesendorp, H. (2021). How is the social meaning of linguistic variation stored in memory? Unpublished PhD dissertation. University of Sheffield. https://etheses.whiterose.ac.uk/29285.

Wagner, P., Trouvain, J. & Zimmerer, F. (2015). In defense of stylistic diversity in speech research. *Journal of Phonetics*, 48, 1–12. https://doi.org/10.1016/j.wocn.2014.11.001.

Watt, D., Levon, E. & Ilbury, Ch. (2023). Accent bias. In J. Beal, M. Lukač & R. Straaijer, eds., *Routledge Handbook of Linguistic Prescriptivism*. London: Routledge, pp. 31–53.

Werker, J. F. (2018). Perceptual beginnings to language acquisition. *Applied Psycholinguistics*, 39, 703–728. https://doi.org/10.1017/S0142716418000152.

Werker, J. F. & Tees, R. C. (1984). Cross-language speech perception: Evidence for perceptual reorganization during the first year of life. *Infant Behavior and Development*, 7, 49–63.

White, K. S. & Aslin, R. N. (2011). Adaptation to novel accents by toddlers. *Developmental Science*, 14(2), 372–384. https://doi.org/10.1111/J.1467!7687.2010.00986.X.

White, K. S., St. Pierre, T. & Johnson, E. K. (2024). In support of varying approaches to the study of variation. *Language Learning and Development*, 20(1), 62–64. https://doi.org/10.1080/15475441.2023.2239787.

Winke, P., Gass, S. & Myford, C. (2013). Raters' L2 background as a potential source of bias in rating oral performance. *Language Testing*, 30(2), 231–252. https://doi.org/10.1177/0265532212456968.

Wojtkowiak, E. (2022). L2-induced phonetic drift in the speech of Polish learners of English: Phonological implications. Unpublished PhD dissertation. Adam Mickiewicz University.

Xie, X. & Fowler, C. A. (2013). Listening with a foreign-accent: The interlanguage speech intelligibility benefit in Mandarin speakers of English. *Journal of Phonetics*, 41(5), 369–378. https://doi.org/10.1016/j.wocn.2013.06.003.

Xie, X., Liu, L. & Jaeger, T. F. (2021). Cross-talker generalization in the perception of nonnative speech: A large-scale replication. *Journal of Experimental Psychology: General*, 150(11), e22. https://doi.org/10.1037/xge0001039.

Xu, Y. (2010). In defense of lab speech. *Journal of Phonetics*, 38, 329–336. https://doi.org/10.1016/j.wocn.2010.04.003.

Zhang, X., Cheng, B., Qin, D. & Zhang, Y. (2021). Is talker variability a critical component of effective phonetic training for nonnative speech? *Journal of Phonetics*, 87, 101071, 1–16. https://doi.org/10.1016/j.wocn.2021.101071.

Zhang, Y. & Wang, Y. (2007). Neural plasticity in speech acquisition and learning. *Bilingualism: Language and Cognition*, 10(2), 147–160. https://doi.org/10.1017/S1366728907002908.

Speech Samples

All speech samples were drawn from talk shows and interviews that are publicly available online:

Speech sample 1: excised from www.youtube.com/watch?v=QgjkjsqAzvo.

Speech samples 2 and 3: excised from www.youtube.com/watch?v=raE87U2TLJo.

Speech samples 4 and 5: see open access data repository: Verbeke, G. & Simon, E. (2023b). Replication data for listening to accents: Comprehensibility, accentedness and intelligibility of native and non-native English speech. https://doi.org/10.18710/8F0Q0L, DataverseNO, V1.

Speech sample 6: Phonologie du français contemporain, available at FLORAL-PFC – Base de données sur le français oral contemporain dans l'espace francophone (projet-pfc.net). For this speaker, see: Coquillon, A. (2010). Conversation à Marseille (Bouches-du-Rhône): Un cuisinier dans la marine. In S. Detey, J. Durand, B. Laks C. & Lyche, eds., *Les variétés du français parlé dans l'espace francophone: Ressources pour l'enseignement*. Paris: Ophrys, pp. 117–129.

Acknowledgements

I wish to thank the series editors, Patrycja Strycharczuk and Robert Kennedy, and two anonymous reviewers for their helpful comments and suggestions. I would also like to thank Gil Verbeke, Chloe Ostiguy and Hanna De Haes for discussion and feedback on an earlier version.

Cambridge Elements

Phonology

Robert Kennedy
University of California, Santa Barbara

Robert Kennedy is a Senior Lecturer in Linguistics at the University of California, Santa Barbara. His research has focused on segmental and rhythmic alternations in reduplicative phonology, with an emphasis on interactions among stress patterns, morphological structure, and allomorphic phenomena, and socio-phonological variation within and across the vowel systems of varieties of English. His work has appeared in *Linguistic Inquiry*, *Phonology*, and *American Speech*. He is also the author of *Phonology: A Coursebook* (Cambridge University Press), an introductory textbook for students of phonology.

Patrycja Strycharczuk
University of Manchester

Patrycja Strycharczuk is a Senior Lecturer in Linguistics and Quantitative Methods at the University of Manchester. Her research programme is centered on exploring the sound structure of language by using instrumental articulatory data. Her major research projects to date have examined the relationship between phonology and phonetics in the context of laryngeal processes, the morphology–phonetics interactions, and articulatory dynamics as a factor in sound change. The results of these investigations have appeared in journals such as *Journal of Phonetics*, *Laboratory Phonology*, and *Journal of the Acoustical Society of America*. She has received funding from the British Academy and the Arts and Humanities Research Council.

Editorial Board
Diana Archangeli, *University of Arizona*
Ricardo Bermúdez-Otero, *University of Manchester*
Jennifer Cole, *Northwestern University*
Silke Hamann, *University of Amsterdam*

About the Series
Cambridge Elements in Phonology is an innovative series that presents the growth and trajectory of phonology and its advancements in theory and methods, through an exploration of a wide range of topics, including classical problems in phonology, typological and aerial phenomena, and interfaces and extensions of phonology to neighbouring disciplines.

Cambridge Elements

Phonology

Elements in the Series

Coarticulation in Phonology
Georgia Zellou

Complexity in the Phonology of Tone
Lian-Hee Wee and Mingxing Li

Quantitative and Computational Approaches to Phonology
Jane Chandlee

Psycholinguistics and Phonology: The Forgotten Foundations of Generative Phonology
Naiyan Du and Karthik Durvasula

Issues in Metrical Phonology: Insights from Ukrainian
Beata Łukaszewicz and Janina Mołczanow

Second Language Phonology: Phonetic Variation and Phonological Representations
Ellen Simon

A full series listing is available at: www.cambridge.org/EPHO

For EU product safety concerns, contact us at Calle de José Abascal, 56–1°,
28003 Madrid, Spain or eugpsr@cambridge.org.

www.ingramcontent.com/pod-product-compliance
Lightning Source LLC
LaVergne TN
LVHW020350260326
834688LV00045B/1651